Cricket's Unholy Trinity

To Emma and Rachel, with love;
and to two of cricket's 'elder
statesmen': Reg Sinfield and Reg Parkin

CRICKET'S UNHOLY TRINITY

David Foot

Stanley Paul

London Melbourne Sydney Auckland Johannesburg

Stanley Paul & Co. Ltd

An imprint of the Hutchinson Publishing Group

17–21 Conway Street, London W1P 6JD

Hutchinson Publishing Group (Australia) Pty Ltd
16–22 Church Street, Hawthorn, Melbourne, Victoria 3122

Hutchinson Group (NZ) Ltd
32–34 View Road, PO Box 40–086, Glenfield, Auckland 10

Hutchinson Group (SA) Pty Ltd
PO Box 337, Bergvlei 2012, South Africa

First published 1985
© David Foot 1985

Set in Linotron Baskerville by Input Typesetting Ltd, London

Printed and bound in Great Britain by Anchor Brendon Ltd,
Tiptree, Essex

British Library Cataloguing in Publication Data

Foot, David, 1929–
    Cricket's unholy trinity.
    1. MacBryan, Jack   2. Parker, Charlie
    3. Parkin, Cec   4. Cricket players—England
    —Biography
    I. Title
    796.35′8′0922   GV915.A1

ISBN 0 09 159830 3

Contents

Acknowledgments

In my research I have gone to relatives, friends and contemporaries of the three subjects in this book. They have generously given me their time, memories and impressions. A refreshing honesty on their part, free from confection and over-sentimental retrospection, has helped and guided me in my evaluations.

I mention Reg Sinfield and Reg Parkin first because I leaned on them most. One Reg was the intimate companion of Charlie Parker, the other was the son of Cecil Parkin. My hours with them were nostalgic joy. I was enthralled by their reminiscences: marvelling at the mighty talents of those days, gasping and chuckling at the authentic stories. It seems right that I should dedicate this book partly to them.

Wherever possible I *talked* to people, to confirm incidents, obtain opinions and gain for myself an evocative feel for the times about which I was writing. Gubby Allen and R. E. S. Wyatt were particularly helpful. High on my list of credits – and, a modest man, he will be astonished to find himself in such august company in another little 'trinity' – must come Keith Ball. His research has been invaluable.

For Charlie Parker, I went to Grahame Parker, Gloucestershire's historian (not to mention erstwhile double-century-maker and manager), retired sports editor George Baker, Andy Wilson, scorer Bert Avery, Professor Francis Berry, Tom Pockett and Peter Legge. My thanks to them all and to Cheltenham Library. I am equally grateful to those who helped me with my reappraisal of Jack MacBryan. Among them were Mrs Cecil Mackay, Nigel Daniell, Geoffrey Cuthbertson, Royse Riddell and Edward Francis (from the Somerset Wyverns), Reg Holway – one of several good enough to show me private correspondence – and Brian Johnston, of eternally chirpy BBC fame. Nor should I forget JCB's surviving sister, Mrs Ivy Hardy.

At one stage I quoted at some length from an article of mine in *The Cricketer*. This will not be viewed, I hope, as self-indulgence. It was the outcome of a visit of mine to one of my subjects and the interview was a valid contribution to my portrait. Statistics are not my forté; nor do I consider they are especially important in psychological studies. But *Wisden* could never be ignored. I have adhered to its facts in a complementary rather than reverential way.

I thank those who lent photographs. They include Gloucestershire, Sussex and Lancashire county clubs, George Baker, Mrs Cecil Mackay, the Somerset Wyverns, Reg Parkin, Reg Sinfield, Richard Walsh, Stephen Green and H. A. 'Ossie' Osborne, Sussex CC's honorary librarian.

There is finally a posthumous element. I am grateful to Charlie, Cec and Jack. They can't answer back, but I have tried to write fairly about them – and always with affection. At times I didn't like them and recoiled from things they did and said. Yet their spunky characters fascinated me. I hope you will respond in the same affectionate way.

Introduction

This isn't quite a cricket book. It is a story of three fine cricketers. There is a subtle and important difference.

Long ago I discovered there was more to life than a game of cricket: and more to cricket than runs and wickets. The book is a reassessment of the feats and careers of three disparate and underrated talents. But the brief I set myself was to study their minds and motives alongside their mentions in *Wisden*.

Charlie Parker, Cec Parkin and Jack MacBryan played their best cricket in the 1920s. It was an evocative epoch. The Australians whacked us as we recovered from the First World War. Our Test selectors had aberrations. There were Hobbs, Sutcliffe and Woolley – and Hammond on the way. Some counties still seemed to parade more kaleidoscopic fancy caps than resolute shots but that only reflected the social tableau of the times.

The amateurs and the pros continued to go their separate ways as they walked off the field. It was simply a microcosm of the British class structure and found a tacit acceptance by the majority of the professionals – though not by Parker, a farm worker's son who had been reading about the Russian Revolution, and not entirely by MacBryan, an amateur who professed to have more regard for the game's paid craftsmen.

Charlie Parker played for Gloucestershire, and only Wilfred Rhodes and Tich Freeman took more wickets. He bowled his left-arm spinners at nearly medium pace. I shall dwell on his marvellous bowling but not to the exclusion of his improvised skills in the art of pugilism and physical altercations even with Sir Pelham Warner. He played only once for England and we shall try to discover why.

Cec Parkin was the Lancashire bowler it was impossible to define. He was a sort of off-spinner, yet such a label is defamatory to him. He started as a quickish bowler and ended at what was good medium pace for someone who turned the ball so much. To the despair of wicket-keepers he was inclined to experiment incessantly, often with six different deliveries in an over. He could spin the ball from leg and was renowned for his comically slow googlie. Indeed he *was* a comic, cricket's 'bag of tricks', whose jaunty antics and handsome grin on that strong face masked an abrasive nature and the misery that was to follow. He was an Old Trafford hero. We'll look at the elation that went with it – and the poignant suddenness of his decline.

Jack MacBryan was, until his death in 1983, our oldest surviving Test cricketer. He, like Parker, played only once for his country. He was a fine opening bat for Somerset. The style was classic and, during the summers he headed his county's batting averages, he was perhaps the most perfectly correct exponent in the country. He was an amateur who spoke his mind. Mostly he spoke out about other amateurs. It wasn't the best way to gain Test recognition.

More and more in my research, I discovered how much my three cricketers had in common.

They hardly knew each other. But they found themselves on occasions playing with or against each other in representative matches. They were generous in mutual praise. 'Parker's a wonderful bowler – I don't know what Gloucestershire would have done without him,' wrote Parkin. 'MacBryan? He's one of us in attitude,' Parker, the pro, used to say.

It wasn't just the others' cricket that they admired. They knew they were similar birds, although one had a flat North Country voice, another caressed rural vowels and a third carried the well-modulated tones of upmarket comfort. They were contrary and perverse. They hated cant and pussy-footing. They were never, whatever the company, inhibited about dispensing invective. And, they were all self-destructive.

Jimmy White, an expansive North Country financier with a minimal knowledge of cricket, was the man behind Rochdale when Parkin played in the league. Cec warmed to self-made men because they didn't really give a toss for protocol. White once went along to watch Parkin playing for the Players against the Gents. During the afternoon, his raucous voice boomed out across Lord's: 'Hey, which are the Gentlemen here?'

There were polite coughs and indignant looks. Parkin chuckled to himself – and approved. So would Parker and MacBryan, for complicated psychological reasons.

The three of them could be bad tempered. But that is altogether too superficial and sweeping. It's of more value to explore the paradox. Charlie was loved by the fellow professionals at Bristol, Gloucester and Cheltenham, even by one wicket-keeper, the late Vic Hopkins who was plucked straight from village cricket at Dumbleton and plunged to distraction as he attempted to comprehend the devious turns, ruthless rambles and short cuts of Charlie's deliveries.

Parkin could upset Arthur Gilligan in a Test match and then have the persuasive charm necessary to enlist the former England captain as the writer of an affectionate foreword to one of his books. He was one of the most magnetic professionals of his day. Spectators, not only those of Lancashire, came specifically to watch him. They giggled at his visual jokes and the bewildering variety of his bowling. He didn't seem to scowl when he was punished. They saw the broad smile: they only read, or heard rumour about, the other side to his nature.

MacBryan was supposedly rude, snobbish and ungenerous of spirit. There is evidence, however much he chose to obscure it in that affectedly gruff and cynical manner of his, that he could be kind and compassionate.

His father ran a private home for the mentally sick and Jack was a frustrated psychiatrist himself. As a sixteen-year-old schoolboy he spent hours with a woman patient who had tried to kill a baby. 'I developed a considerable liking for her, in her plight.'

Long after his own marriage had ended, he sustained a long and loving friendship with a much younger woman who, like that patient, also had a serious mental condition. I was told: 'His concern for her was exceedingly tender.'

Journalistic instinct drew me to all three cricketers. I have long wanted to write about Charlie Parker. I grew up on stories about him and suspected that a third of them were true. It seems to me they all were. Now was the chance to set out his achievements as a spin bowler – and to discover for myself what really did happen in a hotel lift after one of the county's annual dinners.

I went to Blackburn to talk to Reg Parkin, himself a former county cricketer with Lancashire, about his father. I came to know Jack MacBryan well in the last years of his variegated life. The more I delved, the more my 'trio' became intrinsically linked in my mind. All were absorbing characters; all were dogged by controversy of the kind they almost chose to embrace.

Controversy has always been part of cricket. It titillates and enlivens the human fabric. Much of it is unseemly but we are inclined to relish it in retrospect. Journalists get blamed for emblazoning it in black type across the back pages. The hypocrites tut-tut only after reading every word.

Parker belonged to Gloucestershire, from where 'WG' left abruptly after the most acrimonious of committee meetings and the innuendos. Long after, Tom Graveney also packed his bags and walked out. If it was a petulant exit, it appeared to me at the time that he had every reason to make it.

Parkin's Lancashire had a long history and a short fuse. There were tetchy exchanges with Yorkshire and Middlesex just before and after the turn of the century.

Archie MacLaren, once in a paddy, threatened to go off and join Hampshire. Walter Brearley always implied he was on the point of departure. And I haven't started to write of S. F. Barnes's prohibitive contractual negotiations.

When it comes to MacBryan's Somerset, the controversies tower as high as the Blackdown Hills. Didn't the county once restart a fixture against the Australians, on their first visit to Taunton, after play had been called off for the day? The Aussies rapidly curtailed a boozy picnic on the Quantocks and returned to the county ground by horse and trap. And, oh yes, there was the Taunton match against Sussex when the war-wounded last man hobbled out in a lounge suit and just failed to make it in time. And . . . well, what's new about cricket controversy?

My three cricketers are dead and they played the game during decades which I don't personally remember. They can't dispute actions and attitudes which I attribute to them. How much am I entitled to weave my imagination around the factual evidence?

From my days as a sixteen-year-old junior reporter, callow and naïve, when I summoned up enough sagacity not to change my shorthand notes to assist a brash Sunday paper in a libel action it faced, I have retained an obsessive interest in truth and the justifiable interpretation of it.

Alan 'Jock' Dent wrote of the famous dramatic critic James Agate as the Ego diarist: 'He wasn't exactly a liar. But in his writing he was inclined to soar into something which he defined and defended as "the higher truth". It consists in embroidery upon, or elaboration of what actually happened or was said.'

Ryszard Kapuscinski, one of Poland's finest journalists, said the other day in the course of a long interview in the *Observer:* 'What do you understand by a fact? Coal production figures are a fact. But mood is also a fact, and so is human expectation.'

Neville Cardus, a wordsmith without malice, adopted

a somewhat cavalier regard for facts. He knew well enough what his revered employer C. P. Scott had to say about them being sacred. He was too good a *Manchester Guardian* journalist, of course, to get a symphony conductor's name wrong or to miss the accurate details of a hat-trick at Old Trafford. But he couldn't resist telling us just why the musicians were in such a headlong rush to reach the end of the score, or what the successful bowler had had for breakfast.

In his beloved Lancashire dressing room, gnarled old pros would discover what the engagingly verbose Cardus had written about one of them. He'd decorate his prose with splendid, descriptive quotes from the players themselves. 'But I never even spoke to him,' they'd protest, basking at the same time in such a flattering piece of fiction.

Late in his life, the loquacious Sir Neville would readily discuss his evocative journalistic liberties with other cricket writers. 'But, my dear chap, it's the SPIRIT of the thing that counts. Often when I quoted a player in my report, he may not literally have said those things. Then the pause and the smile. 'But he'd have liked to. . .'

I shall no doubt be accused of inventing one or two of the more dramatic incidents involving Parker, for instance. The truth is that I went to great pains to authenticate them. I was also cautious, over matters of mood, in my imaginings.

Cecil Parkin's career was ruined by what went in the newspapers under his name. 'Whenever I open my mouth, I'm in trouble,' he said, without too much sign of changing his ways or mellowing his comments. Cheques from Fleet Street have proved irresistible to many cricketers over the past sixty or so years. One imagines Percy Fender was well recompensed for the reports he sent back during the 1920-21 tour of Australia. The journalistic excursion upset the cricket authorities and some of the players. Very soon, Test players were debarred from this source of income.

Plum Warner was one of several incensed by Parkin's indiscreet dalliance with newspapers. Nothing less than the most abject apology would do in the case of Gilligan, he said with finger-wagging admonition. He wrote that if the imprudent Parkin wasn't careful, he'd be regarded as 'the first cricketing Bolshevist.' What, ahead of Charlie Parker, down in Bristol?

Cardus, never averse to a mildly obscure allusion, called Cecil 'the Jack Ketch of cricket'. He was the executioner of the Duke of Monmouth after Sedgemoor, I eventually discovered. The records imply he needed five chops at the head. A historian friend, with a murky academic sense of humour to complement a penchant for the summer game, suggested that Jack Ketch obviously had a tendency to play down the wrong line. It was something Cec, Charlie and Jack often chose to do in life.

For someone who seemed to thrive on contentious behaviour and be ready to discuss it in print, Cec could be selective. I found little in his own writing about one unpleasant scene in 1920 when he was playing for Rochdale.

During a match in the early season he was so incensed by several decisions given against him by the umpires that he stormed off the pitch. The game was held up until his pique subsided and he was persuaded by his captain to start playing again. It led to his suspension by the Central Lancashire League.

There was an embarrassing impasse as he refused to apologize. Rochdale, no doubt swayed by his considerable ability as a league cricketer and as the best crowd-puller they had ever known, supported Parkin. Eventually, in an atmosphere of huffy compromise, honour was satisfied.

Honour was never satisfied in the case of Charlie Parker. 'Those buggers in high places made sure I'd only play once for my country.' If anyone ever collates cricket's most famous quotations, there will have to be a place for Parker's: 'Mr Bloody Warner will go to bed when I've finished with him.' The incident, mainly confined before now to rumoured implications out of the side of the mouth, is faithfully recorded in this book – though preferably not for those with a nervous and sensitive disposition.

The best and kindest sports editor I ever worked under was George Baker, of the *Bristol Evening World,* who started as a lift boy when Rothermere moved into the West Country in 1929. Two years later he was walking out to open the innings in an evening fixture against Bedminster, one of Bristol's oldest established clubs. 'I was astonished to find that Charlie was one of the umpires. He was my great hero and I was utterly overawed.'

After several overs the bronze-faced umpire patted George on the shoulder. As the fielders changed over, Charlie gently took the bat from sixteen-year-old George and went through the forward defensive shot. He did it without ostentation. The unsolicited advice, given with infinite consideration in a twenty-over evening beer match, made a lasting impression on the young batsman.

Some years later, when Parker had finished playing and was doing some coaching in Bristol, George Baker was talking to his hero again. 'What's the greatest asset of all for a bowler, Charlie?'

The answer came back without hesitation. 'Direction . . . any bowler can learn to spin a ball. But knowing exactly where it's going to pitch is so much more important.'

Cricket grounds between the wars were, despite the hard times – heightened it seemed in Bristol by those stark orphanages – full of characters in the crowd. At Ashley Down there was an old man with a fiddle. He meandered in and out of the spectators with a tune and a song which he artlessly composed himself for every occasion. Out in the middle, Parker, poker faced and cap over one eye, was knocking over castles.

'Give us a song about Charlie.'

Now this Charlie Parker's
A regular old tartar. . .

The metre was suspect and the lyrics undistinguished.
But the instant ditty wafted out from the mid-wicket
boundary to the bowler's end. The cloth-capped crowd
laughed. If Charlie heard, his expression didn't give him
away. George Baker, by now a copy-boy, hurried back
to the office to write a story about an old man and his
fiddle.

Nothing is more revealing, I have often found, than
the conversational shorthand of cricketing contemporaries. 'Charlie? Oh yes, quick tempered, I'm afraid,'
said Bob Wyatt. 'Jack MacBryan? Ah yes, a man of
prejudices,' said Gubby Allen.

Wyatt returned to the Somerset amateur. 'He was
very upset, you know, when he didn't go to Australia.'
J. C. W. MacBryan, as I discovered in my meetings
with him, had no doubts at all about the reason for his
rejection. When Wyatt started playing county cricket,
rightly proud of his bowling, it happened that Mac was
one of his first victims. He made his debut at the beginning of May 1923 against Worcestershire and took a
solitary wicket. Then, against Somerset at Taunton at
the end of the month, he took three more – MacBryan,
Dar Lyon and Charlie Winter, an amateur from Repton.

The memory prompted an observation from both
JCW and RES. 'Well I had already scored 62,' the
Somerset man recalled. Wyatt said: 'My captain,
Freddie Calthorpe noted my successes as a bowler and
told me I couldn't do both. That was nonsense, of course.
I was dropped down the batting order. I got my first
hundred at No 9.'

Background material for psychological studies – of the
kind I like to think my three elongated profiles are –
isn't gleaned in the main from record books. It comes
from snippets of fascinating and unlikely information.
Who'd have thought the fiery Parker would have a
comprehensive knowledge of the Bible and could recite

long sections verbatim? Who'd have thought Parkin liked to leave his pub on a Sunday and go up into the pulpit of a local church, of almost any denomination, 'to speak of sport and God'.

Their attitudes to money provided another eloquent facet to the trio's complex characters. Jack MacBryan liked a bottle of good claret, hosted a party with financial bravado and really had no spare cash to speak of. Charlie Parker was always borrowing from his team mates. Cecil Parkin was called mercenary on occasions and that angered him.

He was a hard negotiator when it came to wages as a league player. He knew his worth and let people know. When he played a Test match in Sydney, he heard that a visiting MP from Lancashire was offering a tenner to any England player who scored a hundred.

'What chance have I got if I go in last?' he asked the philanthropic Member.

'All right then, Cecil. For you a fiver if you get 25.'

There was no hope of an England win as he walked to the wicket. His mind was on the two bowlers, Ted McDonald and Arthur Mailey, and a fiver to augment his appearance money. He told the bowlers. 'What about it, then – there's nothing at stake.'

Mailey was seldom ungenerous in spirit. Perhaps McDonald was already thinking of becoming a citizen of Lancashire. Parkin made 35 and the MP was waiting for him as he came off the field, wallet in hand.

He wasn't a man to miss a financial trick but, as son Reg said, he had a big family to bring up. There was rancour from him because a number of leading Lanca-shire supporters decided not to support his benefit fund. 'Ee, you're too keen on the brass, Ciss,' someone once told him.

Parkin resented any suggestion that he was mean. He retorted, with some justification, that he made 'great sacrifices in time and money', travelling miles around the country speaking at dinners and cricket functions.

Few village clubs, however small, asked him in vain. Never, he claimed, did he ask for any kind of fee.

Unlike MacBryan and Parker, he laughed a lot. He did when he saw George Gunn coming down the wicket to Ted McDonald of all people He did whenever Jack Russell pulled a tin of cough sweets out of his pocket to dissuade Cecil from appealing. (Why is it that Essex has traditionally produced so much fun?) He did, unabashed, when Somerset's Guy Earle hit him farther out of the ground at Old Trafford than anyone else, before or since.

'I went up to him next morning and told him he owed me 4s 6d.' The handsome ex-skipper of Harrow wanted to know why. 'Because I needed a taxi to get the ball back!'

Parkin was well aware of Earle's unsubtle reputation. He regretted that he wasn't in the Lancashire side which went to Taunton in 1926. That was when Earle, as if doing his brutal best to exorcise the nightmarish memory of the famous Eton-Harrow match he let slip, smashed a straight drive through the window of the elevated Dickensian press box.

It was a demoralizing, not to say hazardous, occasion for the Fourth Estate. In the same match Ernest Tyldesley did the same on the way to his seventh hundred in consecutive fixtures. I trust neither was given a glowing write-up. As one adept in trench warfare and evasive action at Taunton, coping with the insensitively directed fusillade of aggression from muscular warriors like Botham and Richards, I know when to be sparing in my prose.

I hope you will detect the whiff of pure humour in my story of three absorbing cricketers. There was Charlie with his classical music, Jack with his embroidery and Cecil with his conjuring tricks.

Yet could there ever have been a more unholy trinity?

Part One
Parker, Charles Warrington Leonard
(1882–1959)

Born Prestbury, Gloucestershire, son of village labourer. Educated Cheltenham Grammar School. Played for Gloucestershire 1903–35. Left-arm spin bowler who took 3278 first-class wickets. Only Rhodes and Freeman took more. Six hat-tricks in his career. Yet he played only once for his country (*v.* Australians 1921).

'Leaving out Parker at Headingley in 1926 was the
most extraordinary mistake in all Test history'
R. E. S. Wyatt

1

No Room for 'Plum' in the Lift

The principal guest at the annual dinner of Gloucestershire County Cricket Club on 19 February 1926 was Mr Pelham Warner, described on the menu card's toast list as the famous England and Middlesex player. It was a splendid occasion for the Grand Hotel in Bristol, and the head waiter hovered with measured obsequiousness. The ancient city's establishment was prodigiously represented. Mr Foster Robinson, the current Sheriff, was there in full civic stature; so was Mr V. Fuller Eberle, Master of the Merchant Venturers' Society, an august and magnificently inaccessible body which, in Bristol, assumed almost regal eminence complemented by a whiff of masonic mystique. The large banqueting suite sparkled with good fellowship under the handsome chandeliers, ornate and welcoming.

At the top table sat Lieut-Colonel Douglas Charles Robinson, Gloucestershire's captain, next to a former skipper of Somerset, Mr Sammy Woods. Sammy, it was said, never turned down an invitation: and there were many extended to the warm-hearted Aussie. His unquenchable laughter reverberated across the room. He had given up leading Somerset twenty years before but the cricketing stories, all without a mite of malice, cascaded from him between the courses. Harvest homes, skittles evenings, county dinners: all were there, he maintained, to be enjoyed. His degree of slightly boisterous

3

conviviality, always acceptable because of the man he was, varied with intelligent discretion according to the gathering. At the Grand Hotel, he privately conceded, there would be no call for one of his hearty tenor renditions.

The county's pros tended to sit together. They used to meet first in a local pub to dispose of a pint or two with practised alacrity. Though they would never admit it, the lubricating exercise was a necessary aid to confidence. The annual dinner, where they were outnumbered by noisy and well-bred committee men and their chums, could be a rather awesome event.

There the professionals sat, in a tight and initially self-conscious group, on that cold February evening – at just about short mid-wicket distance from the top table hierarchy. And as they fidgeted at first with the freshly starched white tablecloths, they made the usual ritualistic jokes about finger-spin when George Dennett caressed the rounded bread roll in his gnarled fist. The rural Alf Dipper, never half as dour as he looked at the wicket, sat alongside the taciturn, popular Harry Smith, one of the best stumpers the county ever had. There was Percy Mills, assuring his mates in that gentle north Gloucestershire burr that he really was intending to decelerate from military medium to off-break: and Bernie Bloodworth, whose sunny nature always found favour with Gubby Allen, reminding his intimates that he could bowl left-arm spinners apart from standing by as the deputy wicket-keeper.

The pros, Gloucestershire's honest journeymen. You could spot them in a flash. Faces still bronzed from the last August sun, and enigmatic eyes that danced with reminiscent humour one moment and became transparently careworn the next. The looming contract, or before long perhaps the lack of one, was always on their minds, increasingly so as the dole queues lengthened in Bristol.

'Not much sign of hunger here,' growled Charlie

4

Parker in censorious tones intended to reach the ears of the company's higher echelons.

If the professionals at the county dinners mostly confined their conversation to incestuous dressing-room jokes and subdued barbs at the expense of the amateurs, two of their number generated attention – for varying reasons. When heads turned towards the pros, the focal points were invariably Parker and Wally Hammond.

In fact, Hammond was missing from the 1926 dinner. He was still out on the MCC tour of the West Indies, steadily beginning to build his majestic reputation, getting bitten by mosquitoes and on the brink of a serious illness which kept him out of the Gloucestershire side for the whole of the 1926 summer. He was in every sense a notable absentee at the Grand Hotel. The sycophants among the membership would have liked to fawn over him; the prettier waitresses inclined to coquetry would have liked him to be there, to wink at them even before the end of the soup course. In the few years since he had arrived at Temple Meads station in mid-winter, protected from the cold by his Cirencester Grammar School scarf, he had started to savour the sniff of emergent glamour. At Bristol Rovers he had already demonstrated that he was by far the fastest winger on their books, though his soccer career was actually a brief and unfulfilled one. He'd earned the envy of more accomplished and established players at Eastville by his success rate with the girls from the old Princes Theatre, his ostentatious arrival by car for training, and his ability to drive a golf ball out of sight.

At the county ground he hadn't yet been dubbed 'The Prince' but his presence at the crease was a matter of mounting excitement. Here, everyone seemed to agree, was a Test cricketer with a long and illustrious future. He walked to the wicket, this son of an army major, as if he already knew his worth. The step carried the suggestion of a swagger; the appearance was immaculate, down to the silk handkerchief which peeped out of the trouser pocket. At Rovers, where his reserve team wages were £2 a week, he lavished five shillings of that on the wife of general factotum Bert Williams – later to be the club's paternal trainer – so that she would do his washing. He rejected the proposed functional club digs to take a room in swankier Clifton. His clothes were well cut. He bought the better seats at the Princes on Monday nights to size up the prospective talent for the week: talent assessed by nubile and sensual standards rather than artistic ones. He probably basked in the envy of his colleagues. He went his own way but could be amusing, even occasionally garrulous, in the dressing room. The conscious desire to withdraw from those he played with, the introspection and the irritating lack of accessibility belonged to the years ahead. In the mid 1920s he was certainly more convivial than arrogant.

At the 1926 dinner when Pelham Warner spoke of the Graces, of Jessop and of Hammond, the twenty-two-year-old batsman was scoring 111 against British Guiana. The distinguished speaker heaped praise on Hammond. He dutifully looked along the top table. 'Colonel Robinson . . . well, yes. . . Here is a fine, intelligent leader whose qualities are widely praised.' He plucked a name or two from the ranks of the professionals. There was not even the most cursory mention of Charlie Parker. The omission may have been accidental; that at least is a charitable view to take.

Parker was forty-three, the elder statesman of the team. He had talked incessantly before, during and after the meal. He ranged from classical music to the Russian Revolution – and even found time to embrace cricket. His words carried the stirring passion and simple eloquence of the self-educated man. He didn't intellectualize. Few in the club were more articulate but the words he used were short and unambiguous. His invective, delivered with a relish that was as calculated as it was fearless, made the wine glasses tremble. Charlie drank strong ale himself.

Plum Warner sat down to prolonged applause. Parker

kept his hands deep in the trouser pockets of his blue serge suit.

The speeches that night were full of pleasant platitudes. Gloucestershire, everyone appeared to be saying, had been the cradle of county cricket with the emergence of the Grace clan. The Sheriff, swayed by the glass-tinkling cordiality of the occasion, went as far as to allow himself unscripted flights of lyrical enthusiasm about the state of the game in the county. He said that signs of resuscitation were evident, though membership was down to fewer than a thousand.

Towards the end of the speeches, in that smoke-filled dining room, the pros were getting just a little restive. They'd had enough of the formality by then; they were ready to stretch their legs and have another pint or two in one of the side bars at the Grand. But their interest was suddenly reawakened when Charlie's name was called out. Colonel Robinson was on his feet. He was holding two silver-mounted cricket balls on an ebony plinth.

'I don't need to tell you why we are having this special presentation,' he began. 'Will you come up here, Charlie?'

Christian-name terms, indeed. That was a rarity – and Charlie Parker stiffened defensively. Then he pushed back his artisan shoulders and walked forward, one hand still in a trouser pocket.

'This great bowler of ours,' went on the Colonel, 'is to receive this memento of his tremendous achievement against Essex last season, when he took seventeen wickets for 56 runs. Well done, Charlie.' The gathering stamped their feet, banged their palms on the table and applauded for almost a minute. There was some good-natured cheering among the pros. No one could have doubted the warmth of the feeling extended to C. W. L. Parker.

There was a pause. He held the memento and read the inscription. In a strong voice he thanked the skipper for his presentation. He hesitated and chose his words carefully: 'It's nice to hear kind words like this about the players – because, I assure you, they heard something very different in the summer when the team wasn't doing so well.'

Parker, with the impeccable timing of an intuitive actor, looked along the top table, detecting with private pleasure any hint of discomfort. The committeemen and their principal guests wondered – and worried about – what he might say next. He was now looking at Plum Warner, without expression or clue to emotions. 'Mr Warner spoke of the coming visit of the Australians and said, if I remember correctly, that England would be "giving the Colonials" a hot reception . . . Well, all I've got to add is that the selection committee would do well not to overlook some of the players in the less fashionable counties.'

Not just counties like Warner's Middlesex, Charlie was daring to say. He had raised his voice in making the point. The tone was more aggressive and challenging than one expected amid the well-polished vowels of a county-cricket dinner in a swish hotel. He glanced at the memento's inscription again. Seventeen wickets in a match – and Plum Warner couldn't find it in his heart to dredge up half-a-dozen words of praise, he thought to himself.

Everyone clapped again, with more polite formality now, as he returned to his seat. 'That's telling the buggers,' whispered a fellow pro.

'Come on,' said Charlie. 'Let's get some air.'

Mr Warner's presence had been something of a coup for Gloucestershire. He was invited back for the annual dinner three years later. What happened at the Grand Hotel in Bristol on the evening of 19 April 1929 has been rarely mentioned since, and only then during indiscreet port-flushed evenings or by old pros who whisper it from behind their beer mugs. As for most club officials, they prefer to think it never happened at all.

As usual it was to be a rather splendid occasion. The Lord Mayor of Bristol represented the city. The county's new president, Lord Sherborne, was at the head of the table. Two hundred males sat down to a babble of bonhomie. The staid *Western Daily Press* reported next morning: 'Geniality was the dominant spirit of the enjoyable gathering.' Perhaps it was as well that the conscientious reporter confined himself to a verbatim report of what went on inside the banqueting suite.

The toast list was again a long and imposing one. Speakers were to include Mr L. C. H. Palairet, Mr P. F. Warner . . . and Mr C. W. L. Parker. Charlie had made it. More significantly to him, he had been granted the elusive prefix 'Mr' to which he argued he was always entitled.

Palairet had captained Repton, Oxford University and Somerset. He scored twenty-seven centuries for Somerset and that county never had a more studiously correct, and at the same time beautiful, batsman. He was a land agent and secretary of the Taunton Vale Foxhounds. The tenor of his speech in Bristol was very much that of the man: restrained, respectful and inclined to be reactionary. The nearest he broached controversy was when he said, of advocated changes in the structure of the game: 'The MCC will only make them I promise you, if it is right for cricket.' Such a conservative view prompted a chorus of hear-hears. Bev Lyon, soon to be Gloucestershire's captain and one of the game's most intrepid philosophers, was ominously quiet. At the next annual dinner – it was still only 1930 – he dared to suggest that Sunday cricket should be tried. By 1932 he was indicting Lord Hawke and all others who sat in judgment. But more of that later.

After Lionel Palairet came Plum Warner, now in his mid-fifties and becoming increasingly set in his ways. Once more he was all affable and controlled charm. He started by telling the Bristol company of the day he was missed by E. M. Grace at point – 'And, by Jove, the Coroner didn't drop many there!'

At some point in most of his speeches he felt it his duty, in a voice that was by nature rather more dull than inspirational, to reassure everyone that there was nothing wrong with cricket. 'It is an imperial and a world-wide game,' he pronounced, and then struck by another thought, he added, 'and d'you know, I've actually been asked to take a team out to Germany this year.'

This ambassadorial gesture evoked an audible ripple of approval. 'Oh dear,' he said in mock reflection, 'I do hope it won't cause another war!'

There is a certain irony in the remark. In his excellent book *Lord's*, Geoffrey Moorhouse includes a non-attributable observation from someone who knew Plum well. He could, it seems, 'make a rather vicious enemy if you fell out with him – it was perhaps this streak that accounted for his refusal to refer to the First and Second World Wars as such; to Warner, they were the first German War and the Second German War. . .'

The rest of Warner's speech at the Gloucestershire dinner was mainly concerned, in complimentary terms, with specific West Country players. His admiration for Hammond was apparently boundless; the distinguished speaker compared him with WG. Wally, bronzed after a recent tour, half looked up to acknowledge the generous tribute. He had other pleasurable things on his mind. The following week he was off to Yorkshire to marry Dorothy Lister, a Bradford wool-merchant's daughter. It was to be a grand, top-hatted ceremony, and he'd asked Herbert Sutcliffe and Abe Waddington to be among the guests. The days of the eligible and free-ranging bachelor were, one concluded, almost over. He was marrying into money. For his part, he was doing it in style: his wedding gift to Dorothy was to be a gleaming new car.

But the sweeping compliment of Pelham Warner dragged Hammond back to cricketing thoughts. 'The West Country must surely be proud of two great cricketing figures in our England XI,' continued the speaker. 'I refer, of course, to Hammond and J. C. White.' He applauded the efforts of some of the Gloucestershire amateurs. Charlie Parker, who had taken 790 wickets for the county in the previous four seasons alone, was utterly ignored. Not an accident this time, surely?

Parker bristled and said nothing. When it was his turn to speak, responding to the toast to the Professionals, he chose to give the evening's principal guest not even a token mention. Charlie was a good deal more forthcoming about other occupants of the top table. He clearly liked the current captain, Harry Rowlands, who came from Cheltenham, almost next door to where Parker had grown up at Prestbury. He presented Harry with a gold fountain pen, from the rest of the team, and listed a few of the qualities he admired in an amateur skipper.

Just before he sat down, Parker suddenly threw in a wily psychological point. This time he did look in the direction of Warner and let others see him do it. 'There's the little matter of a world record that's passed unnoticed.' He had everyone's attention and the theatricality of the situation appealed to him. 'I bowled through the whole of the Worcestershire innings last season and only one run was scored off me.'

Just that. No false modesty, though in truth the records vary slightly from his version. He reckoned he had done something that no one else had managed on a cricket field. And he wanted Pelham Warner to know about it.

Charlie took his seat and allowed himself a deep, eloquent swig from his pint glass. Reg Sinfield patted him on the shoulder. 'Well done, Charlie. That told 'em.' Reg, like all the other pros, was full of pride. He also sensed Parker was a very angry man that evening. He could see it in the face; he had been conscious of the suppressed fury in the great bowler as he sat through the slights contained in the Warner speech.

A few formal pleasantries remained. The little beneficiary Harry Smith was called up to receive his cheque for £1,156 and, in his sheepish way, moved to the president's side with that slightly ungainly gait which

11

suggested he spent most of his days crouching behind the stumps or waddling around at deceptive speed in those baggy shorts on a football pitch. He combined the two – with Gloucestershire, then Bristol Rovers and Bolton Wanderers respectively.

Now it was Percy Mills's turn. He toiled like the honest craftsman he was, always deserving more wickets, complaining hardly at all when stiff-jointed fielders, of whom after all he was one, failed to stoop for reasonable catches as he cut the ball away off amiable medium-pace. Yet here he was taking five Somerset wickets without conceding a run. It was a sweet and rather elusive triumph for him. The mounted cricket ball was presented to him – and Lionel Palairet allowed himself a wrinkled smile.

And with that the dinner was officially over. Now was the time for socializing and more drinking. That usually meant the amateurs with the amateurs and, from choice, the pros with the pros. At the top table the Lord Mayor, civic chain sparkling, was preparing to leave. County officials and Corporation aides fussed around him. Wine waiters still glided past with trays of cognac. Parker viewed the scene with visible displeasure and, we can reasonably assume, some political guilt.

He drained his glass with a plebeian flourish. 'It's too stuffy in this bloody place, Reg. Let's go up on the balcony.'

Sinfield opted tactfully for silence. He followed Parker out of the dining room and towards the hotel lift. Parker had discovered on previous visits to the Grand Hotel that it was possible to go out on the balcony on one of the higher floors – to gaze down on Broad Street and take some fresh air.

Hotel guests were milling around in the foyer and the lift was already filling up. Parker and Sinfield squeezed in. Suddenly the lift attendant was creating a stir. 'Make way, make way,' he was saying with fawning effect. 'This is Mr Pelham Warner. We must have room for him in the lift. Make way, please.'

12

Plum was ready to go to his room and was receiving the VIP treatment, to the apparent detriment of everybody else, of an impressionable lift attendant, especially happy to be subservient when it held promise of a sizeable tip at the end.

Charlie Parker was not going to make way for anyone. His eyes blazed as Pelham Warner gingerly approached the crowded lift cage. It was detonation-point. Reg Sinfield held his breath and even wished he was back playing Minor Counties for Herts. Every person in that lift, men and women in evening dress among them, had the distinct impression that they were about to witness high drama.

The whole incident lasted for no more than thirty seconds. Parker flung his arms out and grasped Warner by the lapels. 'I'll never in my life make way for that bugger. He's never once had a good word to say for me. This so-and-so has blocked my Test match career. I played once in 1921 – and he made sure I'd never play for England again. He even got me up to Leeds in 1926 and then left me out. Make way for him . . .? Mr Bloody Warner will go to bed when I've finished with him.'

The grip on the lapels tightened. There was a nervous hum of agitation from the bystanders. Blows seemed imminent. Warner, always a frail man, said nothing. Here was one of the game's most distinguished figures, a captain of Middlesex and England, a Test selector, founder of *The Cricketer,* cricket correspondent of the *Morning Post,* pillar of the game's establishment, involved in a highly embarrassing public scuffle.

Sinfield knew that all the compounded rage of Charlie Parker was perilously close to ending in blows. If anything Reg, the former Navy boxer with his broken nose and jutting jaw, looked more the fighting man. In truth he was a gentle soul. There was rather more anxiety than optimism in his voice as he said: 'Come on, Charlie. 'Tisn't worth it.'

Parker held on to Warner's lapels for another ten seconds. His hands trembled. According to Sinfield,

Plum was 'as white as a sheet'. Then the grip was released and the county club's famous guest scurried away up the stairs this time, to his room. In the lift cage the easing of tension was actually audible.

'The bastard,' Parker repeated. 'He alone ruined my chances.'

By any standards, in any company, it was an extraordinary incident. County officials learned only by second-hand of what had taken place. There were so many conflicting rumours – even though the scuffle took place in such a public place – that Gloucestershire found it hard to substantiate enough to take disciplinary action against their greatest bowler. Only one of Parker's team mates witnessed it.

I had over the years heard various versions, some more bloodthirsty than others, of what took place on that April night outside the lift of Bristol's Grand Hotel, five days as it happens before I was born. John Arlott, I think it was, over a nocturnal glass of claret, first sharpened my journalistic instincts with a tantalizing whiff of that particular scandal.

Reg Sinfield authenticated it for me in detail. I have softened the physical data and deleted some of the expletives. The rest was as it happened. I imagine Pelham Warner regretted accepting that second invitation to the Gloucestershire CCC dinner. As far as I know, he never once mentioned the incident to any of his friends.

If this evaluation of Charlie Parker appears to be turning into an indictment of Plum Warner, the impression should be discounted. It isn't part of my self-appointed brief. Others have diligently dissected and examined his human qualities, praising his skills and love for the game and maybe offering reservations about his intractibility. As I grew up, a long way from Lord's, there was, to this schoolboy, an odd mystique that surrounded his name. I didn't warm to him: and I daresay it was unreasonable.

After the war I retained vividly the splendidly succinct word picture that Robertson-Glasgow painted of Warner in what was, I believe, his final season as Middlesex's captain. 'Here he was in the flesh, bald as an ostrich egg under his Harlequin cap, slight, small-boned, pale of face, and with nothing but cricket in his conversation.' Crusoe was renowned for his generosity of spirit and an affection for most strands of the human race. Those few, telling lines of how he saw one of the game's most illustrious figures, lines that moulded in my memory like a cold bronze bust, were not, it seemed to me, of the most endearing imagery. Maybe Robertson-Glasgow suspected that Plum, whom he succeeded as cricket correspondent of the *Morning Post* in 1933, was paid more than the nine guineas a week that according to the editor, Howell Gwynne, was the going rate.

Enough of Pelham, more of Parker. He bowled with his cap on, at a defiant angle over his right eye. He bowled with his shirt sleeves dangling, flying in the wind and irritating a few small-minded batsmen. And he bowled like no Gloucestershire bowler, before or since.

He played for the county 602 times, more than anyone else. He took 3,278 first-class wickets at an average of less than twenty. Six times he took the hat-trick, twice against Yorkshire and once against Middlesex in both innings. Against Somerset in 1921 he took all ten wickets; eight more times he took nine. Seven times he took fifteen or more wickets in a match. From 1921 to 1935 he passed 100 wickets in a season; five times he took 200. At Cheltenham in 1930 he destroyed Surrey on his own and gobbled up eight wickets before lunch. He topped the national bowling averages and a great many people, not just the partisans, argued that he was the best of his kind in the world.

That, in a soulless sort of way, is the irrefutable evidence. That is the measure of the man, all the same.

I have no serious complaint with those who take a wary view of statistics. Such figures are preserved for the small print in dreary tomes that fail for ever to stir my pulse rate. But Charlie Parker's innate skills were mountainous, higher by far than the Cotswolds which climbed above his native home. They demanded to be paraded at the highest level – for his country.

As a left-arm spinner he had few rivals. Some pundits claimed he needed a sticky wicket and that, as the most cursory of glances at his career record will prove, was a lie. On a difficult wicket it was almost impossible to play him; on a perfect batsman's track he was 'a damn sight better than almost anyone else around'.

By all the logical yardsticks of the game, assuming that Test teams are chosen by rational and relatively unprejudiced people, Parker should have played many times for England. He played once – and did well.

Again, five years later, he received the august summons to report for the Leeds match against the Australians. As if the gods were on his side, allowing him to take his revenge for previous slights, they rolled out with ethereal mischief a spinners' wicket for him. First there was rain and then the best of Yorkshire sunshine.

The saturnine Parker even permitted himself the flicker of a smile. He impatiently rubbed his fists together. Down in the West Country his pals had heard the weather report over the wireless and were chanting: 'Good old Charlie!'

They were silenced by the ludicrous announcement that Parker had been left out of the side. Arthur Carr won the toss and put the Aussies in. The tourists' dressing room bubbled with astonishment and relief.

There has surely never been a greater aberration on the part of the England Test selectors, bizarre and blinkered as they have often been. Everyone in the game acknowledged that it was an appalling error of judgment. Why ever did they bring Parker all the way to Yorkshire – if they only wanted him to take out the drinks? His obvious rival, Roy Kilner, also caricatured by the way he rakishly wore his cap, this time over his left eye – was in and he had the good grace to blush. The Yorkshire crowd wanted to approve of their own spinner's inclusion but they, too, knew that it was wrong.

Charlie Parker heard the composition of the team and

scowled to himself. He was not given to pussy-footing around with phoney emotions and chivalrous phlegm. He cussed to himself and if there had been a bike slung against the back of the Leeds pavilion, he'd have cycled straight home for a pint of Glevum ale. Some of the other pros murmured their words of sympathy. The Parker face was one of fury.

We shall never know for sure why he was left out. It was not in the remotest sense a decision based on logic. So we can only conclude that grown men allowed their intelligence to be warped by bigotry. There is simply no other explanation.

The other day I was reading again some reflections by Wally Hammond, who after all knew Parker better than most. He wrote of that Leeds Test match and the omission of his Gloucestershire colleague. 'Well, that's how it goes – and Parker never grumbled.'

I have seldom come across such cosmetic tosh. I fancy I can hear Charlie thundering out from the other side of the grave: 'Well, I can tell that's how it bloody well doesn't go. And I'll sodding well grumble as much as I want to!'

Forgive me if I don't pay too much respect to chrono-logical order. I'm impatient to take a more detailed look at that monumental selection blunder. There will be plenty of time later to ponder, rather more dispassion-ately, the other elements of Charlie Parker's absorbing character and cricketing skills.

2

Mockery of Test Match Recognition

The solitary Test came almost by default in the July of 1921. It was perfunctory recognition, ephemeral glory – and for Charlie no more than a kick in the crotch.

He was back from the war, gloomy of feature and fluent of tongue. There was plenty for him to talk about: the human folly and wastage of the trenches, and friends from Cheltenham and Tewkesbury he had lost for ever. He'd twice been turned down by the army himself and ended up in the emerging Royal Flying Corps. But he hadn't been an officer, not like Gilbert Jessop in the Manchester Regiment, or some of the other Gloucestershire amateurs with their pips and their panache. Even George Dennett, that quiet, unpretentious Man of Dorset had crashed through the barrier and into the officers' mess by way of the Somerset Light Infantry.

The war hadn't so much changed Parker as solidified his opinions of life. As part of his developing self-education he read with a ferocity noted by his team mates. The sweeping events of 1917 absorbed his interest. No one ever went so far as to call him a Commie but his admiration for the Bolshevik triumph was never disguised. Charlie's family tilled the soil in their modest way; his sympathy for peasant radicalism was honest and straight from the gut.

And the war had also made him more outspoken, though some would say his invective, when roused, was

18

in the championship class from the day he first took the tram from Temple Meads to the county ground. Before the war, he bowled left-arm fastish. Now, because he chose to – and no one was going to say otherwise – he was slower and more crafty. It suited the persona.

When the 1921 series against the Australians arrived, Parker was already thirty-eight. They were demoralizing days for England. The Australians were gloating, with every reason, over the way they'd beaten England in all five Tests in the winter series; back here, in 1921, three more Tests were to be lost and two drawn. The cartoonists were beginning to reveal a satirical draughtsmanship designed to bruise fragile egos.

No fewer than thirty players were used by England in the series. Sydney Pardon wrote in *Wisden*: ". . . proof that we are not a real eleven but a series of scratch sides. I contend that our cricket authorities played into the Australian hands by treating the Test matches from the first so casually. I have a feeling, amounting to conviction, that they lacked a settled policy. They were inclined to catch at straws . . . Our teams suffered from the casual and unsympathetic way in which things were managed. Men ought not to be in doubt twenty-four hours beforehand as to whether or not they are going to play in a Test Match.'

Sixteen players made their debuts against the Australians that summer. Seven of them, including Gloucestershire's Alf Dipper, Hampshire's A. J. Evans – a prisoner of war renowned for his escapes and the book he later wrote on the subject – and Surrey's delightful Andrew Ducat, who led Aston Villa in the 1920 Cup Final and died at the Lord's wicket during a wartime match, never played for their country again.

There was what almost amounted to surreal resignation on the part of the selectors. One of them was John Daniell, of Somerset, whose detractors claimed he was better at assessing the skills of a rugby three-quarter. The other selectors were H. K. Foster, a former captain of Worcestershire and just one of the seven brothers who remarkably played for the county, and Reginald Spooner.

This was the Spooner of the poetic off-side proclivities. His leaning off drive was among the best of his day; nor was there a more graceful and feline cover point. Lancashire suffered because he was not available more often; so, arguably, did England. We shall never know what his memory was like. Charlie Parker, a gawky upstart from club cricket in 1905, claimed Spooner as his maiden wicket in the first-class game.

Spooner, Foster and Daniell rang the changes in 1921 with indecent, some would say demonic, rapidity. *The Times* was starting to thunder. Leather chairs down in the London clubs were creaking uneasily under the weight of restive MCC members.

The slow bowlers were all being tried. Wilfred Rhodes played in the opening Test. Somerset's Jack White, with a geographical nudge from Mr Daniell, was given a solitary Test. Percy Fender played in two, Cec Parkin (of which much more later) four and Frank Woolley, left-arm slow, all five. And Charlie Parker was summoned from rustic pastures for the fourth Test, at Old Trafford. He and Charlie Hallows were the debutants this time. It could have been almost anyone.

Parker was told to report to Manchester. No emotion played across his face. He sniffed and wondered who'd be left out on the morning of the match. Team mates ambled up to congratulate him. 'Let's see first if I play,' he said with measured cynicism.

It had been a lovely summer. But the rain clouds were around at the end of July. It was a wet wicket and the match was never finished. But Parker was no failure.

Australia, strong of batting, were bowled out for 175. Charlie bowled twenty-eight steady overs, sixteen of them maidens. He took 2-32. Even more significantly, he bowled the majestic Macartney for 13. It was an unplayable delivery on a capricious wicket.

Encouragement from a fellow pro was valued by Parker. It came in this case from Ernest Tyldesley, that

20

unruffled amasser of runs who should surely have played more frequently against the Australians. 'A beauty, that one,' he shouted to Charlie. Tyldesley's generosity was extended when his well-taken catch to dismiss Pellew gave Parker his other wicket.

The Australians were all out for 175. But there was no play at all on the first day and the match never took on a real competitive shape. England had the best of what there was. They declared in their first innings at 362 for four and then bowled out the Aussies for 175.

In the token second innings, with no time left, Hallows and Parkin opened and Charlie was at No 3. He made 3 not out. It was a matter of private pleasure to him that he strode to the crease at first wicket down in his only Test. No one ever dared to tell him he couldn't bat.

Parker packed his bag and pulled on his all-purpose blue serge suit. The pros shook hands and as ever their eyes were eloquent with uncertainty. 'You've done enough for an England run now, Charlie,' someone said.

His lips creased in the merest suggestion of a smile. The face was sagacious and all-knowing without being arrogant. 'You don't know those buggers,' he replied, waving a thick, artisan arm in the vague direction of where he imagined the selectors were sharing a whisky and soda.

Nevertheless he went off back to Bristol in good heart. There was irony in the weekend visit of John Daniell's Somerset. The England selector was at No 7 and Parker got him stumped for four.

They exchanged a glance. Daniell's self-reprimand was tinged with admiration for the guile of the bowler. Parker, indeed, was quite magnificent in that match. In the first innings he bowled just over forty overs and took 10-79. He got through his overs quickly but the word was passed round, in the side streets of Horfield and St Andrew's. Increasing numbers of small, excited faces filled the windows of the adjacent grey-stoned orphanages. In that strange almost melancholic melody of the Bristol accent, the spectators made it clear that Charlie wasn't just a Gloucestershire wizard. He was an England one, too.

Somerset, whose record as a first-class county has been one of crazy contours, still made 212 on the day that Parker took all ten. Jack MacBryan was top scorer; Jim Bridges and Robertson-Glasgow struck some meaty blows at 10 and 11, less at Parker's expense than Percy Mills's.

Percy bowled only two overs fewer than the left-arm spinner. In fact, apart from a couple of overs from George Dennett, Mills and Parker did all the bowling. Mills's figures were: 38-7-116-0; Parker's were 40.3-13-79-10.

Two of the Somerset batsmen were bowled. Archie Young, known to everyone as Tom, that fine and frail professional, was one of them. He resisted skilfully for a long time as he scored 34 and gave support to MacBryan, who alone seemed to have the technique to withstand Parker's marvellous flight and spinning fingers. Louis Wharton, the Trinidad-born amateur, was the other Somerset man to be bowled. He had only a few matches for the county and once hit 86 with a neat little flourish of strokes. But Charlie Parker convinced him, that afternoon at Bristol, that the championship circuit was really no place for him.

A few greybeards still talk about the match and pretend they can remember it. It must have been a wonderful finish. Gloucestershire needed 205 to win on the last day. They lost their first five wickets for 65 but Bristolian Harry Smith – who once kept wicket for England but didn't for Gloucestershire in that particular game – defiantly stayed for two hours and 62 runs. The match went on past half past six and Somerset lost by one wicket. The spectators still went home on the third day rightly talking about Parker on the first.

An England debut . . . and then all ten wickets. Surely the prelude to a long and lustrous Test sequence. Who, gentlemen, are we kidding?

In 1922 Parker took 206 wickets; in 1924 he took 204;

in 1925 he took 222; in 1926 he took 213. Shall we go on? What were the selectors doing or, more pertinently, thinking? Were they oblivious to the reputation he had built as a bowler of mesmeric flight and teasing movement towards the off stump? Maybe they were less oblivious to his reputation for truculence and a propensity to speak his mind regardless of company.

Many an aficionado was baffled by Parker's consistent omission and the Test selectors' apparent rationale. Some of his colleagues in the Gloucestershire side were openly angry. Their attitude was not one of loyalty: rather did it reflect affection. The other professionals, and at least some of the amateurs, loved Charlie – even those he harangued for technical lapses out on the field.

At this distance, it is hard to understand how his massive talents, functional and crafty as the ways of nature on the Cotswold hillsides where he ambled as an inquisitive boy, could be ignored as an England player.

By 1926 the selectors were Arthur Gilligan, Percy Perrin and . . . Plum Warner. The Australians were here under 'Horseshoe' Collins, he of the undeviating straight bat and expressionless face. The first two Tests, at Trent Bridge and Lord's, were drawn. And now it was Headingley.

So far in the series the slow bowling had been left to Kilner, Woolley and Hearne. All the indications were that it was going to be a wettish wicket at Leeds. A Charlie Parker wicket, certainly. He was beckoned to join the Test party and the sighs of relief could be heard reverberating all across the Tewkesbury terrain.

The possibility that he might be left out appeared to cross no one's mind. It was the perfect scenario for Parker's fatuously overdue return to the England team.

Arthur Carr was a bellicose batsman, a loyal ally of Harold Larwood and a contentious figure. A few cynical contemporaries at Notts claimed with excessive zeal that the rows were as plentiful as those violent straight drives. England discarded him as a captain, after the fourth Test in 1926, with what looked rather like summary and insensitive censure. His forbidding and intractable facade was in fact softened by some noble human qualities. But his judgment was suspect.

He found disfavour with many for the way he steadfastly sided with Larwood on the Bodyline issue; but for this he would doubtless have gone on playing longer than he did. His most appalling blunder was in his treatment of Charlie Parker.

Test teams are chosen by selection committees in consultation with the captain. Parker remained in no doubt that Warner, in particular, was responsible for leaving him out at Headingley. The evidence does suggest that the decision was equally, if not more so, Carr's. In any case, it was a lamentable lapse of uncomplicated reasoning. It made one seriously doubt the intellect and imagination of grown men, experienced in the ways of cricket and behoven to put the best available eleven men into the field against the Australians.

It was a stunning and absurd piece of selection. According to R. E. S. Wyatt, it was also 'the most extraordinary mistake in all Test history'. That is what he says in his book, *Three Straight Sticks*:

The day was such and the wicket was such that the England captain, A. W. Carr, after winning the toss, sent Australia in to bat. Yet Charlie Parker, the best left-handed slow bowler in the country, was left out of the side. England paid for it by watching Australia score only six runs short of 500 and, after their own first innings, having to follow on. If the pitch justified sending Australia in to bat, it certainly justified including Parker.

This is what E. W. Swanton wrote in *History of Cricket*:

It was Carr's calamitous decision to put Australia in that proved the vital move; or rather, it should be said the combination of this offensive gesture, for which in itself there was plenty to be said, with the decision

24

previously made to stand down Parker. To leave out the most destructive left-arm spin bowler in the country and then invite the opposition to bat on a wet wicket, argue in conjunction a startling lack of judgment or liaison, or both.

In *The Cricket Captains of England*, Alan Gibson points out that Parker's omission was a committee decision, though Warner had assured us in *Cricket between the Wars* that Carr had the last word. Gibson goes on:

The reasons why Parker played only once for England are clear enough to anyone writing, as I am, from the West. He was a poor fieldsman and a difficult man. Nevertheless, there is no doubt that he was at the time and for some years before and after this event, the best slow left-hander in the country. If it was thought proper to invite him to the ground, it was an act of lunacy not to play him when you had decided to put the opposition in because it was a wet wicket. Macaulay could bowl on soft wickets but the passage of years does not make the decision any more rational.

Wisden, while lending its weight to the general condemnation of Parker's humiliating omission, said this of poor Macaulay, used it seemed by some as a convenient scapegoat. 'He failed. A lifeless performance in the trial game shaking any confidence in his powers which the selection committee might have entertained, he was not chosen for either of the first two Tests; and at Leeds, even if he played an invaluable innings, he crumpled up badly before the fierce onslaught of Macartney.'

The cricket correspondent of *The Times* revealed a penchant for additional research:

An inspection of the pitch on Friday afternoon showed that the unprotected part of it was almost marshy. The selectors would have to face one of the most horrid problems which has ever confronted persons in authority. They must have their team finally chosen before the captains tossed and without foreknowledge of the possible vagaries of the weather, and they must choose three out of five bowlers to assist Kilner and Woolley.

Another pitch that was specially prepared for the match was chosen – and then Mr Carr held a consultation in the middle of it, at which two local experts, the groundsman and Sutcliffe assisted. A few minutes later the captains tossed and Mr Carr sent Australia in to bat.

If ever in the last twenty-nine years appearances have justified that policy, this was the occasion. The sun was shining fiercely on a damp marled wicket and the weather seemed to be set fair. But there would seem to have been some lack of co-ordination between the captain and his colleagues of the selection committee, for it was illogical to omit Parker and subsequently put the other side in.

The sawdust was plentifully spread on Saturday morning but Mr Macartney very soon transformed Macaulay's glee into gloom. The estimate of the probable behaviour of the pitch, by whomsoever it was formed, turned out to be ludicrously inexact, for not a ball popped, not a ball broke sharply all day. Batsmen found conditions ideal for run getting. They did not need the protection of batting gloves and the ball rarely gathered pace from the pitch, but came on to the bat fast enough for the purposes of all the scoring strokes ... Macaulay was reduced to complete impotence in two overs. He would overpitch a ball by a foot or so and see Mr Macartney step out of his ground to hit it first hop against the sight screen.

In print and conversation, the latter an art form of prodigious anecdote, Neville Cardus readily returned to the Headingley theme. Caustically, he observed: 'Charles Parker played for England only once, though he was trusted to go out with the drinks in 1926 when Charles Macartney scored a century before lunch on a wicket which would have suited Parker's spin down to the ground. He was one of the most vicious of left-arm spinners I have seen in a long lifetime – the others Blythe, Rhodes, Verity and the Australian Ironmonger. Each not only turned the ball savagely, but caused it to rise at the acute angle of turn.'

Charles, indeed: how strange and alien that sounds. Maybe Cardus, who could be the most unstuffy of companions to the pros, especially to those who shared his northern roots, preferred not to affect chummy intimacies with those he knew less well.

Back in Bristol, the night presses rumbled with partisan resentment. The *Western Daily Press* asked the most fundamental question of all: 'If Parker cannot play in these conditions and circumstances, when *will* his claims be considered?'

The region's morning paper, which devoted a good deal of space to cricket, was unequivocal on what should have happened. 'Chapman should have been left out and Parker included. It was a grave tactical error to omit the first man to get 100 wickets this season.'

I come now to Warner. In *The Fight for the Ashes*, he writes:

The Test at Headingley provoked much controversy, especially on two points. First, Parker who was on the ground, was omitted from the final selection. I need only say with regard to this that Carr had exactly the side he wanted, and preferred Macaulay to Parker. It was thought that the Yorkshireman, on his own ground and before his own people, would be inspired to great bowling achievement. The anticipation was not justified in the result. But if he failed completely as a bowler, Macaulay proved himself a great-hearted and skilful batsman at a time when every run was of untold value to England.

It doesn't sound a very convincing argument to me. The shifting of blame to Carr for final team selection seems hard and gives the impression that Plum was anxious to ease himself out of an argument that had smouldered for too long.

Before the Leeds Test, Parker had played for the Players against the Gents at the Oval. He bowled beautifully in the second innings to take 4-29. Warner was there; he loved these fixtures almost as much as life itself. He watched the Gloucestershire man bemuse the best of the game's amateurs. He knew as well as anyone what C. W. L. Parker could do on a drying wicket – almost without trying, it appeared. Yet the famous selector was a party to the England team's ill-advised composition.

One might have expected a more impassioned compendium of scorn from Wally Hammond, who crouched in the slips in telepathic triumph with Parker. He was the admiring witness to the bowler's craft of cunning, one delivery after the next. He shared many an hotel breakfast table with Charlie, and listened to many an erudite lecture on the game's refinements from him. Hammond, better than most, knew Charlie's worth to the county and the country.

Yet in his autobiographical book, *Cricket My Destiny*, published in 1946, he dismissed the contentious Leeds fixture in a few lines. 'His presence, I still believe, would have won us the match.' We hoped in vain that he would pursue that view. Am I being uncharitable in wondering whether he was inhibited by the fact that Sir Pelham Warner had been asked to write the foreword?

Long after he had given up playing and was then coaching at Cranleigh, Parker received a social call from Andy Wilson, the quiet, popular and, some would contend, the most competent wicket-keeper ever to play for Gloucestershire. When Andy arrived in the West Country ('in a snowstorm', as he used to remind us with that gentle smile of his) from the Lord's staff in 1936, Charlie was the county coach. They always got on well: the superficially lugubrious six-footer and Wilson, not much taller than the stumps. Andy used to bowl left-arm slows and still did so in the Bristol nets to help out,

Charlie Parker (left), for once without the famous cap, and New Zealander Charlie Dacre, a Gloucestershire team-mate

Reg Sinfield, a close and trusted friend

Wally Hammond and Charlie, a deadly duo on the field but rather wry companions off it

Gloucestershire County Cricket Club in 1924. Back row: H. Smith, N. Hobbs, A. E. Dipper, J. Bessant, T. Goddard (in trilby), W. Hammond, P Mills, B. Bloodworth. Front row: G. Dennett, B. H. Lyon, D. C. Robinson, R. G. Rogers, Charlie Parker. Note the youthful Hammond

Studies of the Parker bowling action: expression as set as the cap

Charlie (front left) next to his favourite amateur, Bev Lyon, in the Gloucestershire side which figured in the famous tie with the Australians in 1930. Back row: R. G. Ford (12th man), B. Bloodworth (scorer), A. Dipper; E. J. Stephens, C. Dacre, R. Sinfield, W. R. Hammond; W. L. Neale, C. J. Barnett, H. Smith. Front row: C. Parker, B. H. Lyon, F. J. Seabrook, T. Goddard

It's cold weather as Gloucestershire go out to field. Left to right: R. Sinfield, T. Goddard, W. Hammond, C. Parker, B. Lyon

The Gloucestershire team which beat Yorkshire by nine wickets at Scarborough in 1934. In this group: B. O. Allen G. W. Parker, B. H. Lyon, R. Sinfield, C. Parker, D. A. C. Page, W. L. Neale, C. J. Barnett

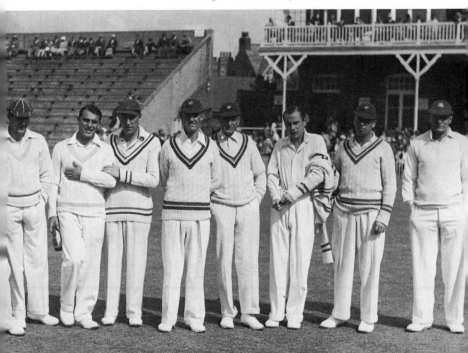

though no doubt rather overawed in the presence of the Master of the genre. As a coach, Parker – in the way of many great bowlers – took a profound interest in the art of batsmanship.

'Who taught you to hook like that, young Andy?'

'Patsy Hendren, Mr Parker.'

There was the grunt of approval. Wilson couldn't have had a better tutor.

The Gloucestershire coach may have been in stern-looking appearance a trifle forbidding for the bright-eyed newcomers. But most of them warmed to him. They got used to his wry sense of humour:

'Now look, son, that won't do, will it? Why don't you use your feet more?

Wilson knew the reprimand was fair. 'I'm waiting for the half-volley,' was his good-natured response.

'Well, I don't bowl any of those, son!'

Gloucestershire's new stumper was hungry for knowledge on the game. His confidence increased in his relationship with the coach. There were plenty of friendly asides. One day during the April nets, as they shared their sandwiches, he asked: 'Tell me, Charlie, when did you set an attacking field?' The retort was immediate. 'As soon as I saw the batsmen coming down the pavilion steps.'

All the professionals, as one can't tire of saying, liked Parker. So it was the most natural thing in the world for Wilson to call on him in his Cranleigh days. The greeting was as genuine as ever. The reminiscences were numberless. And eventually they got round to the Headingley Test of 1926.

It was a subject not openly discussed in the dressing room back in the twenties and early thirties. It was what you'd call now a sensitive topic. The clear but unspoken policy among his team mates was to let it rest.

Now Parker was ready to talk about it. His attitude to injustice as he saw it, whether to another pro or himself, hadn't mellowed. 'Not long before the match I went into the players' lavatory. Warren Bardsley was

29

also there and he told me the wicket was made for me. I told him I wasn't playing. He was astonished and couldn't wait to rush back to the Aussies' dressing room to tell the others. They just couldn't understand it.'

We can just imagine those thick Bardsley eyebrows arching in disbelief. The left-hander had already scored 193 not out in the Test at Lord's; he wasn't relishing the prospect of competing with Parker on a turner at Leeds. Bardsley was by then forty-three but he moved with the speed of a clean-living freshman as he suspended his call of nature and sped off with the tidings that the England selectors had gone mad.

After Headingley, there were two Tests to go – and the Ashes were won surprisingly by England. Carr was to be discarded in favour of A. P. F. Chapman when it came to the decisive Oval match. But this is primarily a story about Parker.

He was in the squad again – even though such a relatively modern term as 'squad' wasn't used in those days – for the fourth Test at Old Trafford. Macaulay and Percy Chapman (doubtless to the satisfaction of the *Western Daily Press*) were dropped; Ernest Tyldesley and G. T. S. Stevens were in. Stevens had plenty of backing where it counted. He had progressed quite spectacularly by way of University College School, Oxford and Middlesex. To impressionable schoolboys he was already something of a national hero. Once he'd scored 466 not out in a house match. He'd earned an early invitation to play for the Gents. He was tall and good looking and in danger of being treated, briefly, as a kind of matinée idol. Apart from his batting, he bowled leg-breaks and googlies very well indeed.

Warner admired him but had some reservations, especially about his fielding. He once wrote: 'Stevens is potentially a fine player but he is inconsistent. . . As a fieldsman he is a safe catcher in the slips, but elsewhere he is slow in moving to the ball and he does not throw well. His spin bowling was a definite asset in both the

1926 Test matches in which he played. At Manchester he bowled well – certainly he looked the most difficult of the England bowlers. And whatever his inequalities at the Oval, he got rid of Macartney, and rendered inestimable service to his side.'

Well, Stevens may have been in but Parker was out. For the Gloucestershire man, rejection was becoming an irritating habit. 'Just as well not waste my bloody time,' he huffed.

Wilfred Rhodes was actually recalled for the Oval Test. Parker had no complaints about that. In moments of extreme intimacy, in the corner of a bar long after play, he conceded that Rhodes was his superior. Some, of course, would dispute it. Comparisons were inevitable: they were two of a kind and yet technically they differed. When Gloucestershire played Yorkshire, Parker became engrossed in the rhythmic economy of Rhodes's action, and the sheer nagging perseverance. Wilfred was forty-eight when he was brought back to win the match and the 1926 series. His 4-44 was bowling that to York-shiremen, and many others as well around the country, was romantic and sublime. They say no match gave him greater joy.

It was in some ways an odd-looking team to win a Test: one with Rhodes and Stevens. Many unwisely thought Wilfred was past it. How were they to know he could still take 100 wickets in a season when he was fifty? Stevens struggled to spin the ball at the Oval and yet produced the best delivery of the match to account for the magnificent Macartney. Rhodes, dour and North Country, probably liked Stevens, posh and southern. Once Stevens dropped him three times in a row. What was that Warner said about his fielding? Such benevolence from a dozing gully deserved everlasting gratitude from Rhodes.

In the next few years, Parker's statistics remained formidable indeed and we shall be examining them later. They made the minimum of impression on Lord's. If the selectors decided he was a bad bet, it must have

31

been on the grounds of social graces – although heaven knows, he could articulate as well as most of the public school cricketers that played in the same era. Parker himself was resigned to the patently unfair fact that his Test career had come and gone in the blinking of a watery and wary hierarchical eye.

Yet there was nearly a postscript to confound everyone. The Australians were back in 1930. England had won the first, Australia the second. The next two were drawn and now it all depended on the Oval, hardly for the first or last time. It was the time for Mr Chapman to be shown the door, with no more delicacy than poor old Arthur Carr had been shown four years before. Bob Wyatt was the new captain.

And for this final Test, suddenly the West Country was astir with conjecture. Charlie Parker, ostrasized and forgotten, was in the named Test party. He was forty-six and well on the way to 179 wickets that summer. Rhodes had been forty-eight.

Cricket writers pleaded his case. Down in Bristol everyone was asking: 'They can't have selected him this time unless they intend to play him, can they?'

He packed his bag with extra care and put in one of the two bats he still bought every season as an optimistic incentive for scoring the elusive 1,000 runs. He took the Great Western to Paddington and met up with the rest of the players. Everyone talked about how Woodfull's Aussies could be beaten. Charlie arrived at the Oval and sensed the tingling atmosphere already created by an expectant crowd.

His bag remained unopened as the players waited to learn who was in. Parker was not.

Wisden shared the opinion of many of the national and provincial papers:

Even at the risk of weakening the batting, Parker who had been asked to be present should have been included, for there was nobody in the side able to bowl the ball going away from the batsman which, as was shown time after time during the tour, was the one best calculated to cause trouble to Bradman. . . The bowling, too, apart from that of Peebles, never looked really good enough to get Australia out at reasonable cost.

Bradman was, of course, the dominant genius with a double century. The Australians scored very nearly 700 to put them into an unassailable position and well placed for the innings victory. The batting strength of the Australians was both vast and ruthless. But ironically it was a left-arm spinner who destroyed England in their second innings. Hornibrook, who was apt to go through a metamorphosis from quickish seam to controlled spin, took seven wickets.

That was it. No more infuriating, false hopes for Parker, no more monumental slights. Ah well, he seemed to be saying, stuff the lot of 'em!

In his book *Three Straight Sticks*, R. E. S. Wyatt was to say: 'Maybe it was a mistake to leave out Parker but it's hard to prove these things. Certainly in the match immediately after the Test, Gloucestershire secured an amazing tie against Australia, largely due to Parker's bowling. But it must be remembered that the pitch at Bristol was very different from that at the Oval.'

I rang Bob Wyatt at his Cornish home to prompt a retrospective opinion on the luckless Parker. His memory was sharp and perceptive; he was helpful and approachable, just as he had been when some months earlier I heard him, with almost sprightly good humour, talk to a cricket society in Bath. He still has the bronzed face of the batsman in high summer.

The 1926 omission? Yes, of course, that was an awful blunder. And what about 1930 at the Oval, when Wyatt himself was the new skipper of England?

By the time he was put in charge, the Test squad had been chosen. He had no say in that; he was presented with the list of names. 'But yes, I suppose the final decision to leave Parker out was mine. And yes, I think it was probably the right one.'

There was no pompous verbal flurry on the part of the man on the other end of the phone simply to justify what had been done more than half a century before. At the same time he implied that he would not have changed his mind with the benefits of hindsight. The answer was not a dogmatic one and I gained the impression that he remained, up to a point, open-minded about the virtues of his (and the committee's) judgment immediately before that final Test match.

'Charlie Parker was a magnificent bowler, you know,' went on Wyatt. He paused before completing a sentence which I assumed had already finished. '. . . if the batsmen let him'. This vulnerability of the spinner, expressed by a contemporary, was too good to let go.

'He didn't like to be attacked. You had to know how to play him. I think I did. I used to go after him. Move down the wicket, if I could, and hit the ball back over his head. No, he didn't like that. It could affect him. His next delivery might be short, then. His length might suffer. Wally could get quite irritated when a batsman attacked Charlie and he lost his control as a result.'

It was a streak of fallibility that surprised me about Parker, the bowler renowned for imperturbability when wheeling away, and steadiness of length.

Wyatt remembers captaining Parker once or twice – 'probably at Scarborough or even in a Test trial'.

So what evidence of that truculent and prickly reputation? 'He was certainly quick-tempered but I didn't find him difficult. One had to treat him gently and encourage him. We had a number of chats together and he once told me he thought he'd scored 50 against every county.' Maybe that was only an ambition of Charlie's and Bob Wyatt misunderstood him. In fact, despite the Gloucestershire man's eminently serious approach to batsmanship, he never quite managed that far-flung achievement. He'd have dearly loved to.

He'd have equally loved to play many more times for England – despite the grunts, towards the end, of seeming indifference. He never forgave those he was convinced blocked his way.

In the context of Test match rejection, there is one final incident to relate. It concerns the only time that Parker fell out with Lyon. Unknown to the bowler, the resourceful captain had made arrangements for Anglo American Oil Company to place their private aircraft at the county's disposal, and to rush Charlie from Croydon aerodrome to Cheltenham, if he was left out of the England side, so that he could play against Leicestershire in the August of 1930.

Lyon was actually at the wicket when, amid some excitement, the plane circled the College ground. It then dropped a message onto the nearby road. Play was held up while the weighted note was passed to the Gloucestershire skipper. Parker had declined the offer because he had never flown before and, in any case, he hadn't learned of his Test omission until just before 11 a.m. that day.

The reaction of Lyon, who had relished the sense of drama and publicity in such an unprecedented air-dash, was uncharacteristic. He made a public statement in which he said: 'I cannot understand Charlie's action – I thought his enthusiasm would be sufficient for him to take advantage of any means of coming to Cheltenham. We are in the running for the championship and could have done with him.'

But it was Bev Lyon who was criticized. 'To question Parker's loyalty, editorialized the *Gloucestershire Echo*, 'is not quite the "cricket" which we have always expected from Mr Lyon and it would have been better if all this had been left unsaid. . . Poor old Charles seems to be loved by nobody. Dropped out of the Test, he is now castigated by his own county captain.'

A fractured friendship was, we understand, quickly restored.

Bowling Genius –
With Two New Bats

The human texture is so rich that I am in danger of allowing the Man to obscure the Cricketer. That will never do. My own quirky obsession with the game's psychological treasures must be curbed. The castles Charlie Parker knocked over were not, after all, exclusively off the field. It is time for me to redress the balance.

This can best be done by a brief, evocative journey, season by season, from his Old Trafford county debut in 1905 to his last game for Gloucestershire against Middlesex at Cheltenham in 1935. Enough of hearsay and harangues; it is now right that through the encounters and the voluminous statistics we should pay our retrospective homage.

He came into county cricket by way of Prestbury CC and Tewkesbury, where the thick-armed Alf Dipper also learned his trade. Parker bowled quickish medium-pace and when the north Gloucestershire air was sticky, he found he could swing the ball. In truth, although nominally he later became known as slow left-arm, he was never really slow. He pushed his deliveries through rather faster than Derek Underwood, when he is at his busiest and briskest for Kent.

Bert Avery, the Gloucestershire scorer whose copper-plate record books resemble works of art to such an extent that you gaze at the delicately penned patterns and come later to the wondrous deeds that they document, is as precise as he is good natured. It isn't simply that Parker played 602 matches for his county; it's the stunning fact that he sent down 151,849 balls – or 25,308 overs. His average was 19.43. He took ten wickets in a match ninety-one times. He was the first bowler to take six hat-tricks; Doug Wright went on to emulate this between 1937-49. That will do for the moment and we shall be returning to his superb bowling.

He would wish us to take an equally serious view of his batting, his captaincy and even his career as a first-class umpire. Dare I add, with a certain roguish delight, his approach to fielding too?

I have already referred to his ritual of turning up with two new bats every season. It was a whim of his that the bats seldom had a black handle. He believed he was quite capable of scoring 1,000 runs in a summer but, of course, never managed it. His style was orthodox and relatively correct. He didn't subscribe to the notion that batsmen towards the lower end of the order should be expected to slog. One season, when the Gloucestershire team arrived for a game in Kent, they won the toss and were falling over themselves to get the pads on. It was a flawless batting wicket.

Suddenly, Parker's strong West Country voice dominated the dressing room. 'I'm going to ask the skipper if I can open.' It took the rest of the pros by surprise, on two counts. One was that he appeared to be getting above himself, assuming that he was now an opening batsman. The other was that he was bothering to ask his captain for permission. For some benevolent, probably end-of-season reason, the captain agreed. It must have been Harry Rowlands or Bev Lyon, not Basil Allen.

Charlie strode out to open the innings with Reg Sinfield. 'He played remarkably well and as far as I can remember it was one of his best knocks. We'd all heard him talk for hours about the way to play the fast bowlers and spinners. And here he was showing us,' recalls Sinfield.

Parker's high regard for his prowess as a batsman was

something of a discreet joke among his team mates. They regularly chortled to themselves, just as long as he was out of earshot. At the same time they realized he had an impeccable grasp of batting theory and they guessed, correctly, that one day he would make a marvellous coach – whether at the nets in Bristol, or at Cranleigh.

It was another away match with Kent when he delivered an early-morning lecture on the unnecessary frailties of the Gloucestershire batsmen in attempting to counter the leg-break cunning of Tich Freeman. 'It's the same nearly every season – he runs through you like a dose of salts.'

'But he's a good bowler, Charlie. Just look at the wickets he gets every year.'

Charlie glared with almost benign pity at some of the more established batters in the side. 'Ah well, 'spose I've got to show you how to do it.'

They held him to his boast. The order wasn't reversed on that occasion but there was plenty of time and scope for Parker to meet – and master – the wizardry of the little spinner. Freeman didn't get a lot of bounce and Charlie, eyes alert and nose not so far from the ground, crouched to smother the spin. There was an immediate googlie and it came up to meet this tutor-batsman. He was hit between the eyes. Shortly after he was out and returned to the pavilion – with 'two splendid black eyes' and an expression of unmitigated anger.

One of the professionals, surely new to the staff and still unversed in self-protective lessons of tact in the presence of the Tewkesbury Tiger, asked with naïve mirth: 'What was that you were saying, Charlie, about how to play Tich?'

The instant response was a violent one. Parker's new bat, of which he was inordinately proud, was sent crashing through the window.

Professional captains were not elected in those days, of course. But he was the senior pro and there were several occasions when he found himself leading the county. He had obvious qualities for the job. Fellow professionals would follow him to the ends of the earth, or even more devotedly suffer vain chases to the fine-leg boundary for him on sweltering July afternoons. He was a man of authority; his words carried respect. He wouldn't have any truck with opponents who patronized his logic and believed they could outwit him with sweet words. And he wouldn't be coerced into compromise to make things easier and more acceptable for an amateur skipper.

On one occasion at Trent Bridge the wicket was offering nothing at all for the bowlers. Gloucestershire were batting and accumulating runs at their own pace. Parker was captain and was happy to keep cool, away from the blistering heat. In any case, it seemed reasonable enough to bat on.

During the tea interval, a perspiring Arthur Carr leaned across to Parker. The tone was overtly affable, the sting was in the eyes. 'When are you going to declare then, Charlie?'

'Don't think my bowlers are in need of any practice this evening, Mr Carr.'

The cosmetic smile had now gone. 'All right – but just wait until next year. We'll have a surprise or two for you.'

And so they had. The Carr memory was long. Trent Bridge had been turned into a flier. And Larwood was steaming even as he walked down the pavilion steps.

Alf Dipper looked at Sinfield. 'Who's going to take the first over, Reg?' Ex-boxer Sinfield stroked his protruding chin in a gesture of unconscious symbolism. 'As it comes.' As it came was that Dipper, the taciturn countryman, went to the far end – and had to face Larwood. There was no gentle range-finder. The first delivery was fearsome. It reared and took the peak of Alf's cap. The ball went for four byes and first slip, standing well back, nearly caught the cap. Dipper called down the wicket: 'For God's sake, get down this end quick!' It carried the urgency of an impassioned prayer.

Gloucestershire were given a thoroughly uncomfortable game. Their own pace attack, by comparison, was risibly inadequate. It was in every sense a victory for Arthur Carr. The tea party twelve months earlier had not been one for skipper Parker to cherish. 'Bloody amateurs. . .' he kept repeating to himself as the train steamed back to Gloucester.

I must not shirk the issue. It is time to examine Parker the fielder. The role was not his forte. He was inclined to move, according to some of his contemporaries, rather like a carthorse. From choice, he didn't indulge in too much running. 'I'm a bowler, not a bleedin' fielder,' he would say when he stooped and the ball went past him.

In Grahame Parker's admirable history of the county club, he recounts the most famous story of all about Charlie – in the context of fielding. Someone hit the ball to leg off Parker's bowling and after an embarrassing delay, with a trio of fielders appearing to leave the chase to each other, they set off in comic unison. Dipper, Dennett and Mills: they sound like a vaudeville act and so they looked that day. Their athletic style was quaint and cumbersome. They might have thrown out a foolhardy challenge to a tortoise.

Parker stood, hands on hips, at this scene transported from the Keystone Cops. 'There', he pronounced in despair after a period of exasperation, silence and eventual merriment, 'go my greyhounds!'

It was, of course, a thankless job fielding to his bowling. As colleagues used to say: 'Wherever the ball went, he wanted you.'

At Cheltenham, Sinfield spent the whole of the morning at square leg. He hardly had a ball to stop but it gave him the chance to chat away with the umpire, Frank Chester, an old friend of his. Just before lunch, the ball curled away to fine leg. Sinfield went after it and returned it to the wicket-keeper. He spied the ominous Parker pose, hands on hips. 'Reg, don't you realize, I want you at fine leg – not square.'

Umpire Chester rallied with good humour to the

fielder's aid. 'He's been standing alongside me all the morning, Charlie, and you haven't moved him.'

In the twenties and thirties, when socially and politically there was so much to fret about, camaraderie was strong on the cricket ground. Struggling batsmen were given half-volleys, maiden century makers were helped on their way with a wink from the bowler. Old pros showed nervous novices on the other side where they were going wrong. We don't often see it now.

Reg Sinfield learned the art of flight by simply watching Somerset's Jack White. In 1938 he took eight wickets against the Australians and two other catches were put down. At Lord's he took the first nine against Middlesex. 'Laurie Gray was still there and he couldn't really bat. Tom Goddard was bowling wide on purpose. Then I turned one down the hill against Laurie and got him on the pads. I didn't appeal. Frank Chester was again the umpire. 'You should have called, Reg. I'd have given him out.'

The rough-grained comradeship was valued in those days. For their part the players seldom showed dissent. There were good and bad umpires – and glares down the wicket when bad decisions were given. It is a revealing insight that Charlie Parker, whatever his reputation as a gruff and at times grumpy cricketer, rarely questioned an umpire's decision. Nor was he a loud and frequent appealer. He was inclined to leave that sonorous plea to Tom Goddard. Gloucestershire indeed never had a better or more distinctive shouter than Tom. His burring, belligerent appeal doubtless ascended the Cotswolds and the distant Malverns as well.

As an umpire, Parker was unmoved by the most vociferous of challenges from bowlers whose sense of judgment over lbw appeals was so often blurred by the scent of personal triumph. He did his job with unsmiling efficiency, shook his head reprimandingly at shoddy batting – just as he did when playing for Gloucestershire – and, in the view of one friendly contemporary, displayed a faint bias in favour of bowlers.

41

He stamped on any hint of gamesmanship; at the same time, he knew from his wide experience of the game that it was easy to come to a wrong conclusion.

Members of the Gloucestershire team used to cite a game against Essex, when Dipper was out just before lunch. In came Hammond, soon to face Hipkin, whose first ball was an enticing half-volley. Wally didn't pick it up perfectly but the ball still skimmed murderously in the direction of cover point. Laurie Eastman somehow held on to it.

There was a hearty collective appeal, orchestrated by Johnny Douglas. They were clearly surprised that Hammond stayed in his ground. The umpire, after a contemplative pause, ruled that it had been a bump ball. Douglas was very annoyed, more so when the great batsman went on to make a big score. At the end of the day's play the Essex captain put his head round the Gloucestershire professionals' door.

'Where's Hammond?' There was no reply. Douglas didn't spot him. 'Well, perhaps you'll let him know that I consider he's got some sauce. That had to be a catch. Everyone knows it was.' And away he stormed, the amateur boxing champion, outraged by what he saw as a clear case of gamesmanship or even cheating.

Hammond still said nothing. Next morning, when it was Essex's turn to bat, he made an unambiguous request to his captain, Harry Rowlands, a peace-seeking Quaker, that he should be given a long bowling spell. This in itself was a surprise. Hammond was the classic case of the bowler who preferred to stand in the slips. From choice he was under-bowled and the county consistently lacked pace attack as a result.

Parker peered up from under that familiar, faded cap. He sensed a dramatic day's cricket ahead. I go back to Sinfield again for a vivid, first-hand memory. 'I'd never seen anything like it. Wally bowled like a demon. He gritted his teeth and made it clear he didn't want to come off.' The atmosphere was taut and unyielding. The kindly Rowlands was no doubt wishing he'd gone to a meeting of the Society of Friends instead. Charlie was even grinning to himself as he witnessed the vengeful scene from the mid-on sanctuary. He mused on what a fine and combative bowler Hammond would have made, if he had wished. One point had been devastatingly made. No one called Wally a cheat.

Diversons are over. I can put it off no longer; I must now write of Parker's bowling. No, of course it isn't an afterthought. But with Charlie there are so many anecdotes, so many whims to side-track us. Did I tell you of the peculiar, almost eccentric, way he took his catches? No. . . no. . . I have promised to come to his bowling, the craft that brought him 3,278 first-class wickets, a record only surpassed by Rhodes and Freeman.

Writing in *The Cricketer*, Aidan Crawley – of Oxford and Kent, of Labour and Conservative party membership – rightly saw the twenties as the Golden Age of Spin. The Australians, he pointed out, produced Armstrong, Mailey and Grimmett. England had a galaxy of stars, including the left-handers Rhodes, Parker, Verity and White. There were the off-spinners Jupp, Clay and Goddard; and the leg-spinners Stevens, Freeman, Robbins, Brown, Marriott, Peebles. . . Dick Tyldesley was, according to Crawley, in a class by himself since 'in spite of every indication to the contrary, he never spun the ball at all'. The list is a long and imposing one, and there are a few omissions. It is pointless to ramble nostalgically through the names of all those leg-spinners and regret again that the breed is now virtually extinct.

Crawley has this to say of the twenties' spinners: 'Charlie Parker, on a sticky wicket was without doubt the most difficult bowler I have ever met.'

That was a widely held view – and not everyone qualified such lavish praise by implying he needed that sticky wicket. Many of his finest performances were on pitches that offered him grudging help, if any at all.

The pedantic technician would contend that Parker

spun the ball better than he flighted it. There is some evidence, sketchy though it is, that just occasionally an intrepid and experienced batsman could hit him off a length. It's an indisputable fact, confirmed by many players of the day, that Jack Hobbs was one of the very few able to face Parker almost every time with complete composure. The bowler, not given to public self-analysis, was honest enough to confide in a barside corner that he was less assertive when wheeling away at left-handers.

His action was beautifully rhythmic and the arm snaked up from obscure mischief behind the body till it became high and imperious at the moment of delivery. There was nothing jerky or ungainly from a man who spurned any inducement to become one of nature's graceful athletes. If he hesitated mentally to contemplate a subtle change of pace or line, the hestitation was never once apparent in the leisured run-up.

Not many spinners, I would dare to suggest, summoned up more aggression over after over. He looked for a wicket every ball. He set his own field and over-ruled, or by-passed, a succession of Gloucestershire captains. This wasn't arrogance, even if one or two of the amateurs would have preferred to see him put in his place occasionally. The sensible skippers let him get on with it.

Douglas Robinson was inclined to assert his military bearing. He really should have known better. 'No, no Colonel, I don't want the bugger out there – I want him in here!'

Always he was watching out of the corner of that cunning countryman's eye, to make sure there was no subterfuge to revise the field again with a quick motion of the hand. If a fielder wavered from the spot – and that meant the square foot – where he had been deliberately placed by Parker, he was subjected to a remorseless tirade of rebuke. 'Make a mark on the ground and bloody well stay there. You've got a catch coming.'

He knew when it was time to go on – and when it was time to come off. He didn't need the skipper to tell him. 'Give us me sweater,' he'd say to the umpire. That was it: then, not before, was the moment for the captain to ponder his bowling change.

When he first arrived in Bristol in 1903, soon to have a try-out against Mr Grace's London Counties at the Crystal Palace, he bowled in-swingers. He used to watch George Dennett getting more luck with less energy. Dennett, a gentle man first brought into the side by Gilbert Jessop, also showed more patience in a single afternoon than Charlie did in a lifetime.

After the war, Parker had it all worked out. From now on he was going to be a spinner and saw himself as the natural successor to Dennett, who in his own splendid and underrated career took well over 2,000 wickets for the county.

Charlie knocked on the secretary's door. We aren't quite sure what ensued. There are various apochryphal and light-hearted versions. Perhaps we can delicately paraphrase the ultimatum. 'I've decided to change my style, sir. I'm going in for slow bowling from now on. And if you don't like it, I'm packing me bags.' And, of course, he never packed his bags.

Nor, I repeat, was he especially slow. He liked to push the ball through. He was a nagging, accurate, THINKING bowler. Grahame Parker likened him, in that aspect, to John Mortimore, the post Second World War off-spinner who pondered away to such an extent that you could almost hear him thinking as he walked back between the deliveries.

There was a mutual affection between the two Parkers, Charlie and Grahame. It transcended the quaint and often insufferable barrier that kept the pros and amateurs apart. They used to travel up together in the train from Gloucester to Bristol. 'I dropped a catch off him at Cheltenham and he sounded off for a moment or two. Then he smiled. I made up for it at Dudley. I was fielding in the deep and hung on to three catches in the same over when the slog was on. I can still see Charlie beaming at me.'

45

We are coming to the end of this reassessment of a great left-arm spinner and we mustn't forget that brief season-by-season journey. His first and only wicket in 1905 was that of R. H. Spooner; he didn't play at all the following summer. In the next eight seasons, up to the 1914 war, he took 454 wickets. *Wisden* reported that he was under-bowled. It also reported that he was inclined to be expensive. He'd had enough of swinging the ball for a living.

Dennett was still away with the army in India when it came to 1919. Parker had made his conditions and was working on his technique to justify them. The matches lasted two days only that season. Left-handers got hold of him on occasions. But he did take sixty-nine wickets, only two fewer than in his best season so far, 1909. 'Charlie's getting the hang of it,' said the Bristol and Cheltenham pundits.

'Course I bloody well am,' was his unspoken response by 1920. The Gloucestershire side was a poor one, badly balanced and indifferently led at times. The remarkable fact is that they won eight matches. A perusal of the scorebook provides a graphic explanation. It was, in effect, Parker who won the majority of those eight games. He took 125 wickets at less than sixteen runs apiece. Against Leicestershire, he took fourteen wickets at just over four runs each. By the end of the summer he was ninth in the national bowling averages. The pundits down in the West Country had revised their assessment. 'He's GOT the hang of it.'

In 1921 both he and Dipper played once for England and were then discarded for ever. For Gloucestershire, he and Dennett did most of the bowling. Their stamina and accuracy were prized virtues. They often had to keep going because the county had a painfully inadequate back-up of bowlers. Parker never noticeably tired during his lengthy spells; to him 'fielding weren't much cop' when you could be pitting your skills directly against the batsman.

His season's tally was 156 wickets and he moved up

to eighth in the national averages. By now his earlier aspirations as a medium-paced swinger were forgotten. It could be argued that his rise to Test eminence had been achieved, in the context of his spin bowling, over a markedly short period. *Wisden* was now chronicling his progress with increasing attention: 'In combination with excellent length, he constantly makes the ball do something in the air, and he has at his command the left-hander's break back.'

Wisden was becoming lyrical by 1922. Old habits die reluctantly and he was still being described, significantly, as a 'left-handed medium-pace bowler'. That wouldn't have pleased him too much. Were they blind to his spin and flight? But the praise was extravagant – and thoroughly earned. He'd taken 206 wickets, after all, at little more than fifteen runs each. He'd sent down 1,296 overs. And he was by now fourth in the averages. For Gloucestershire, *Wisden* assured us, it was 'emphatically Parker's year'. In addition, he played for the Rest of England against Yorkshire at the Oval, and for the South against the North at Eastbourne.

It was also his benefit year. As we've already noted, he never really seemed to have much money. Material things, he would tell his evening colleagues in the course of a political homily, weren't all that important, provided you had enough to pay the wife her housekeeping and had enough left over to buy a couple of bats each year, and a pint most nights. The benefit cheque of £1,075 was nonetheless a welcome one.

His benefit match was truly memorable. The attractive opponents were Yorkshire and the venue had to be switched because of administrative problems at the College, from Clifton to Ashley Down. Charlie Parker's performance over those August days took Bristol's cricketing enthusiasts to elevated levels of ecstacy. What did Charlie do, then? 'He hit the stumps five times on the trot, that's what he done,' was for years the chorused response.

Well yes, Yorkshire still won; but that isn't the point.

47

The great visiting county were bowled out for 66 in the first innings. Parker was unplayable. I extract the bare bones of this enthralling scenario from Grahame Parker's history: Charlie Parker had been engaged in one of the greatest bowling performances in the history of the game. By his seventh over he had taken four wickets. With the last ball of that over, he clean bowled Norman Kilner. Unfortunately, the first ball of his eighth over had also hit the batsman's wicket but had been called a no-ball. With each of his next three balls he clean bowled Macauley, Dolphin and Waddington, to claim his first hat-trick. He had hit the stumps five times in succession.

He finished with 9-36 in just over ten overs in that first innings. It was stunning, magnificent and utterly ruthless bowling. Could there also have been a latent showman's streak after all in the Parker persona? This was his special match, his benefit, and he was going to decorate it with the trappings of his rare and bountiful talents. The apparent balance of the match – or maybe the strong ale dispensed by the beneficiary – was altogether too much for Gloucestershire. They got themselves bowled out for fifty-eight in the second innings . . . and lost.

By 1923 he was one of *Wisden's* Five Cricketers of the Year. The accompanying tribute delved back to Tewkesbury days and thoughtfully referred to F. G. Healing 'who taught him practically all he knows about bowling, and after a time recommended him to the Gloucestershire committee'.

Here, surely, is a valid observation contained in that unsigned article: 'He must at times have bewailed his luck in playing for a county so weak in batting. No matter how cheaply he got the other sides out, he could seldom hope to be rewarded by victory.' The writer, like so many others, couldn't apparently make up his mind about what kind of bowler Charlie really was. 'He is not strictly speaking a slow bowler . . . the batsman thinks twice before jumping out to drive him.'

There were 172 wickets for Parker that season, a

reduction it is true. Yet only Maurice Tate, Cec Parkin and Alec Kennedy, with his ever-willing in-swingers and leg-cutters for Hampshire, took more. The undeniable fact was that Gloucestershire, for all sorts of pragmatic reasons, were still over-bowling him. He affected to complain from time to time and said it was ruining his figures.

The summer of 1924 was a wet one. That probably worked in Charlie's favour. Against Middlesex, his haul was fourteen wickets. In all, he took 204 wickets (av. 14.27). Tate alone took more, one more. It is worth making one or two random comparisons for that season. Jack White captured 147 wickets, Roy Kilner 145 and Tich Freeman 167.

Tests passed Parker by. But he was an automatic choice for the Players against the Gents at Blackpool in September. They used to say he could summon up added aggression in his bowling when it came to outwitting the amateurs. He took 4-70 and 3-20 in that match. The atmosphere was usually relaxed by September; he was said to be talkative and benign. The eyes even twinkled: he was more tongue-in-cheek than chip-on-shoulder.

Apart from the MCC 1924-25 tour of Australia, a team went out to South Africa under the Hon. L. H. Tennyson, as we have already heard. Both Parker and MacBryan were included. They came from different worlds and got on well.

As we shall discover by the end of this book, they had a surprising amount in common – even though Charlie was no linguist, had no time for stockbrokers and never drank port after dinner. The common bond was a matter of attitudes and temperament.

There were five unofficial Tests on that South African tour. Parker played in all of them and took only eleven wickets. In those days, too, visiting sportsmen were effusively entertained and the politics were kept well out of sight. That is unlikely to have satisfied Parker, radical and inquisitive. His bowling was a good deal less composed than normal. He did best on the matting wickets. And he did best of all, irrespective of the opposition, in the very first game, against a Western Province side from the schools and colleges. He had a hat-trick and retired tactfully from the attack when he had taken six wickets for one run in four overs.

Back in Gloucester, during the 1925 summer, he claimed seventeen wickets against Essex and needed only one more for a world record. He bamboozled one batsman after the other. He remained poker-faced, cunning as a Severn Vale fox. Parker in full cry was intent on destruction; there was no sentimentality as he strode forward towards the coup-de-grace. His countryman's bag was 222 wickets, spaced over 1,512 overs (av. 14.91). He played for the Players at Folkestone (5-42), the Rest of England against Yorkshire, the Champions, and for the Hon. L. H. Tennyson (6-101) against A. E. R. Gilligan's XI. It was a plentiful season for him.

Some said 1926 was not a good year for him. He took *only* 213 wickets and the average was up to 18.40. In the public prints, one sentiment recurred. 'He's being called on to do an enormous amount of work, far more than is wise at times. He is having more bad matches for Gloucestershire than is usual.' Loyal West Countrymen would hardly subscribe to that view. No other Englishman took 200 wickets. By now, Wilf Rhodes was down to 115. At Blackpool, Parker played against the Australians and took 5-76 in a thoroughly impressive first innings performance.

By 1927 the Gloucestershire committee were panicking about the lack of well-balanced bowling strength. The message had at last reached them that too much was expected of Parker. Embarrassing bowling weaknesses were compounded when the big heart of Percy Mills let him down at last. He tried in vain to keep going after an injury in the opening match; he didn't play again until the middle of June. Parker himself was struggling with ill health and painful dental treatment. He was no hypochondriac and willed himself to

beaver away as the county's principal bowler. It's astonishing indeed that he could still take 193 wickets. No
other bowler apart from Freeman (181) sniffed that total.
Ponder on the 95 of Jack Hearne, the 86 of Kilner and
the 85 of Rhodes.

Geographical allegiance must not wholly sway me. In
1928, Tich Freeman, just over five foot tall, tugged at
his baggy trousers in that characteristic manner and
mingled his triumphant top-spinner with the other
optical illusions and tricks from his repertoire. He shat-
tered teams on his own and took 304 wickets. Parker
was down to 162. The next season his total dropped
again to 138; in Gloucestershire, Tom Goddard, with
his bucket hands and prolonged bass-like appeal that
suggested he was in ill-advised training for the Three
Choirs Festival, had temporarily surged ahead that
summer with 184 wickets.

Parker's anti-climactic recession, still personally all-
conquering unless measured by the mighty standards
he had already set, could perhaps be attributed to the
unyielding rigours imposed by playing for Gloucestershire. But by 1930 he was back, second in the averages.
H. E. Roslyn wrote in *Wisden:* 'He has never proved so
deadly. Indeed at times there was something positively
uncanny in the way he lured batsmen to their destruction.' At Cheltenham, the tents were deserted and occupants craned their necks at the boundary's edge as
he took sixteen Middlesex wickets and fifteen Surrey
ones.

This was also the year of the famous tie between
Gloucestershire and the Australians in Bristol. Charlie
had a few things to prove. Not for the first time he
produced the theatrical impact for the occasion. He and
Goddard opened the bowling in the second innings.
Parker bowled Bradman and ended with 7-54. He and
Goddard, two six footers, were heaved on to the spectators' shoulders and carried in triumph from the wicket
to the steps of the pavilion.

There never has been a more thrilling or romantic

match in Bristol and, rightly, the details are still recited: the way Jim Seabrook pulled off the best catch of his life to dismiss Grimmett, the daring leadership of Bev Lyon, the miserable batting of Gloucestershire in the first innings and the grandeur of Hammond in the second.

. . . And the classic off-the-cuff comment of the grinning, exuberant Lyon as he reached for his faithful trilby before leaving the still throbbing Fry's ground: 'Any skipper can win or lose a game against the Aussies. But there aren't many who can bloody well tie one.'

Parker captured 179 wickets in that 1930 season. He was roaring up once more with 219 (av. 14.26) in 1931. Apt to be a slow starter, this year he had passed 100 by mid-June and had equalled Hearne's record of 100 by 12 June set in 1896. He was forty-six and the joints were getting stiff. The suspect mobility in the field was even more suspect but no one ever mentioned that. Some thought he was slower in the way he transported his guileful deliveries down the track but he wouldn't have agreed with that.

From 1932 till 1935 the understandable and gradual decline of an ageing and over-bowled cricketer was increasingly evident. He leaned more on the cooperation of a favourable track. Flight had suddenly become less an art, and length an ally. He took 134 wickets in 1932, 119 in 1933, 117 in 1934 (he was fifty years old) and 108 in his final season of 1935.

When Somerset came to Bristol in 1933 there was more benevolence than he'd ever shown to them before as he gave away 20 runs in his first four overs. Maybe he was then goaded by thoughts of what he had done against his West Country rivals in 1921 when he devoured ten wickets in an innings. For the next forty-five balls in that 1933 match he took six Somerset wickets for 2 runs. 'Don't think I'm goin' to be put out to grass yet, you old buggers,' he told them.

His last game was at Cheltenham against Middlesex in 1935. Hammond scored a century, Charlie Barnett chased to 78 off the front-foot and Gloucestershire lost by four wickets. Parker laboured for three wickets and they cost him rather more than was good for the liver. Fred Price was his final victim.

Parker came off the field, knowing in his heart that it was all over. He was not a man to make any sort of emotional farewell. He was cross that Middlesex had won and that he hadn't done better: competitive till the end.

In a Cheltenham bar that evening a Middlesex supporter who had had too much to drink and was gloating over the win irritated Parker more and more. The boorish visitor's eyes were probably too glazed to see the danger signs. He continued to bait one of the country's most distinguished bowlers, now in his fifties and by late evening affected by the realization that his cricket was over for good.

Sinfield, loyal as ever by his side, knew instinctively that the Parker fuse was shortening. He thought of half a dozen occasions. He thought of the lift-cage at the Grand Hotel in Bristol. And he was too slow to diffuse the situation. The noble, old bowler could take no more insults. He was on his feet. He had the incoherent baiter 'by the scruff of the neck'. A yeoman blow sunk into a gross beer gut.

Reg turned to Charlie and said gently: 'Let's be on our way.' Parker, who never suffered a fool, whether in high or low station, in a committee room or the corner of a tavern, drained his glass and walked out with dignity.

'He asked for that, Charlie.' Parker nodded. He'd played his heart and his limbs out for Gloucestershire over thirty years and he wasn't going to hear a bad word said about them now.

4

Loved at Least by the Pros

The prosaic facts are that Charles Warrington Leonard (some records maintain it was Lennard) Parker was born at Prestbury, not far from the present Cheltenham racecourse, on 14 October 1882. It was a farm-labouring family, thick in the arms and with complexions that belonged to the open air. There were nine children and never too much spare money. It was a matter of necessity that the children did their share of physical work. This they did with varying degrees of enthusiasm; Charlie's brand of enthusiasm was one of grudging acceptance that some filial responsibility had to be demonstrated in the agricultural tradition. Like another great West Country cricketer born in a farming community, Harold Gimblett, Parker was not enamoured with the idea of too much hard work. The father, Len, known in the village as 'Blossom', was a general labourer who once fell out of a walnut tree and broke his leg. The family home, at Queenswood, was ironically known as 'The Workhouse'.

There were some bright children in the family as the other villagers began to notice. Once the evening chores were done, the Parker boys and girls were encouraged to pursue their own hobbies. There was a sensitivity, probably inherited from the mother, and an independence of spirit. Daughter Maud showed an aptitude for music and the Parkers made sure she took lessons; she actually went on to become a most proficient musician. Most of the children did reasonably well at school. Charlie had one brother nicknamed 'The Poet' because of his way with words. Another brother, Rusty, was almost good enough to play cricket for Gloucestershire.

Young Charlie betrayed few emotions. He was a rather glum-looking boy, 'a deep one', as they said around Prestbury. He won a place at Cheltenham Grammar School, where his dour exterior would soften with a dry, surprisingly adult, wit. Everyone got excited when one of the old boys, Gilbert Jessop, eight years older than Parker, was selected for Gloucestershire. He'd played for the Grammar School 1st XI when he was only thirteen. His propensity for daring, unorthodox and often brilliant shots at every conceivable angle from the bat, were first paraded in schooldays.

Jessop had left Cheltenham for a probationary teacher's job at Alvechurch when his father, a doctor, died. Parker would occasionally see him back in Gloucestershire but they came from different backgrounds, artisan and professional, and had little in common, apart from an interest in cricket. And as far as cricket went in those early days, well Charlie could take it or leave it. Golf, now, that was different. . .

His brother Arthur had quickly discovered that playing golf was more fun than tilling the land. He ended up as professional at the Cotswold Hills Club. Charlie, never noticeably short of self-confidence, reckoned he was just as talented as Arthur. There is plenty of evidence that he could have been. Grahame Parker tells me he was a near-scratch golfer. Certainly cricketing team mates feared the challenge. For them, there wasn't much future in the wager.

The notion of becoming a golf pro appealed to Charlie. As Arthur told him, they weren't paid much. But there were tips and other perks – and, if you played at Cleeve Hill like Arthur, plenty of bracing Cotswold air to breathe into your lungs. Charlie didn't relish clubhouse ritual but out on the fairways he could swear as much as he wished. During his career as a county cricketer, golf remained the second obsession of his life (along with politics, that is!).

He was inclined to spend many days in the winter, spring and autumn playing golf. One contemporary said: 'That's why he never seemed to have any money. He preferred golf to finding another job.' It was said with affection.

There were always keen golfers among the cricketers. The best, sometimes from other clubs, would take him on – and part with their fivers.

Wally Hammond was a splendid golfer. When approaching fifty, Parker would still compete gamely with Hammond's prodigious swing. His putting carried all the meticulous care and deliberation that he brought to those unflagging stints as a spin bowler.

Soon I shall be discussing that stunning partnership of Parker and Hammond, bowler and slip, a predatory pair who refined the art of destruction with no more than the exchanged slant of an eyebrow. For the moment there is their joint golfing adventures to chuckle over.

The famous one-drive challenge at the Cheltenham ground, following one of the Festival matches, has been retold by Grahame Parker with a graphic prod by Phil Woof, whose grandfather was Billy Woof, generally accepted to have been the first of Gloucestershire's slow left-arm bowlers. It was the late twenties and Parker was tired of hearing about Hammond's golf driving. 'One of these days, we'll see. . .', he was apt to say.

The prospect of such a contest filled mischief maker Bev Lyon with glee. Lyon was renowned for keeping the dressing room happy and mixing with the pros. He was also renowned for imaginative schemes on and off the field. Now he and his colleagues wanted to find out whether Parker could actually out-drive Hammond. Most of them privately hoped he could but they were too realistic to be confident.

The cricket match was over and most of the spectators had gone home by the time the two players solemnly walked with their drivers to an extreme corner of the College ground. It was estimated that there were a good 300 yards to the far opposite end. Wally's drive pitched

nearly out of the ground. He pocketed his bet and said:
'That's one thing sorted out, then Charlie.'

That was one bet the canny older gambler should
never have struck. Perhaps there was more than a touch
of vanity involved. Hadn't he heard of Wally's reputation, for heaven's sake?

At Bristol Rovers, where he used to arrive for training
by car – banger though it was – to the astonishment
of his more mundane colleagues, the golf clubs were
invariably in the boot. The other players at Eastville
used to travel to the ground by tram or on push bike.

One day he initiated a bet and placed a golf ball on
the centre circle. He sent it steepling out of the ground
and, as extravagantly promised, onto a gasworks bridge.
The ball went straight through the open door of a work-
men's hut and landed on the lap of a startled mainten-
ance man having his sandwiches. Bert Williams, later
to be the club's trainer, swore to me it was true. Didn't
news of that feat reach Parker?

This chapter is an attempt to look at Charlie, the
broader man and perhaps to understand him a little
more. And we come up all the time against the
contradictions.

In no sense would one call him a sentimentalist. In
his almost dismissive way he had no time for domestic
small talk in the dressing room. His wife, an attractive
woman, was not often mentioned although she did
attend county matches occasionally. It's hard to see him
in the role of doting father. He was never soft-hearted
about opponents.

If that tends to make him sound a thoroughly unattractive man, I hasten to redress the marshalling of such
relatively superficial facts. He apparently had a good,
working marriage. His children were brought up
according to a strict and affectionate code. He was loved
by fellow professionals, surely the most eloquent of arguments for a good nature, however hard he sometimes
tried to obscure the trait.

At Cranleigh, where he was coaching, he lived in a

council house at Wyphurst Road. The neighbours liked him in his quiet way. The boys at school responded to his kindly guidance. He used to walk to work through the fields and it got around that he'd 'once been a famous cricketer'. Not many were quite sure how famous or whether he'd actually played for England. He liked a morning chat on the way to work and would go along to the Common on occasions to watch the local team play.

No, of course he never made much money from the game. It wasn't in his nature to go hell-for-leather on a winter job like a few of the other Gloucestershire professionals who had big families to support.

But not a sentimentalist? How can we be sure? There are numerous reports of how, after the death of his wife, he knuckled down to looking after his son and daughter. He was too proud and independent to look around for any help. He got the meals and washed the clothes. He was father and mother, and he clearly did it very well.

His attitude to money and worldly possessions coincided roughly with his political beliefs. 'There's plenty around in the world and it's a damned shame it ain't evened out better.'

The professionals got £7 for a home match and £9 for an away one. They had to pay their own expenses out of that. As the shop steward, Parker successfully got them a better deal. The secretary's office at Bristol usually had an intimidating military-like presence about it. Parker would bang on the door and stride in. He knew what he was worth and he spoke up on behalf of more subservient team mates.

'Not that old Charlie ever had any loose cash in his own pocket,' I was told by one who knew him well. 'He was always on the cadge. It was 'Hey, Tom, lend us a few bob till the end of the week,' or "Hey, Reg, can you help us out for a few days." They'd fund the next couple of rounds.'

Reg Sinfield remembers a match at Clacton. A number of the wives went along and Mrs Parker made one of her rare appearances at a game. 'Charlie was never too flush. After this match, he came up to me and told me he was broke and he wanted to get a meal for his wife and himself on the train going back to Bristol. I put my hand into my pocket and pulled out a few, assorted coins.'

In one sweeping movement, Charlie had transferred all the coins to his own eager palm. 'That'll do, Reg, old son.' And he was off back to his wife.

Sinfield pondered again, many years later, Parker's comic thrust towards the cluster of modest coinage. He laughed out loud. 'I'm only grateful I had my own wife with me that day. She was able to get me home!'

For all that doleful countenance of his, Parker could be fun. In his last season, 1935, cricket was really no laughing matter for him. He was past fifty and the beads of sweat dotted his nut-brown brow. The arm wasn't up so high. There were only three wickets against the South Africans in the extraordinary match that Gloucestershire won.

But Charlie threw back his head, above that weary body, and roared with belly laughter on the day that Sinfield was dive-bombed. The players were suddenly distracted during a match when a group of swans came across the pitch. The swans had neither an affection for the game of cricket nor a rudimentary knowledge of decorum. One circled above the hapless Sinfield and off-loaded an excessive deposit of excreta. Play was held up as the embarrassed fielder surveyed the extent of the damage. 'I got a hundred in my next match. Then a 200. Then a hundred against the South Africans. All the time Wally was saying to me "Whatever you do, don't change those flannels. They're bringing you luck." And I kept them on till the end of the season.'

Parker allowed himself the flicker of a smile when there were comic, unconscious antics in the field, just as long as the catch went to hand in the process.

At the Wagon Works in Gloucester, both Andrew Sandham and Surrey were going well. Hammond was crouching at short gully and Lyon was at slip. The ball was turning without bringing success to Parker. He paused, chin in his hand and contemplated. Then very deliberately he beckoned Grahame Parker up from deep mid-on. 'Get in there between 'em', he said. Sandham leaned on his bat and watched the operation; he wasn't going to fall for that. And yet, with almost the next delivery, he was deceived by the spin. The ball flew away, faster than you would have expected, at an angle of forty-five degrees behind the wicket. Maybe forgetting that a new man had just been brought into the arc, Hammond dived one way and Lyon the other, in a vain attempt to take the catch. Young Grahame Parker, more used to running like a stag around the outfield to earn his inclusion, held on triumphantly to the ball. Wally and Bev were collapsed in a contorted heap on the ground. That also brought collective mirth, orchestrated by the saturnine bowler.

Charlie wasn't averse to a little black humour, too. In a home fixture against Hampshire, the bowler was in the mood for experiment. He had his own ideas on how to winkle out the big stodgy left-hander Phil Mead. He waited till Mead had taken guard, pulled on his peak and gone through the other obligatory ritual. Then he revised his field. He decided on three short legs, Wally forward and Bev backward. Again the summons went out in that strong rural voice to the enthusiastic and boyish Grahame. 'Short square . . . no, closer than that . . . And a bit closer.'

The young amateur was no coward as he'd proved on the rugby field at full back for Cambridge and England. But by now he was two yards from the bat. 'It's all right, old Phil can't hit hard,' someone hissed.

Charlie's first ball was, for him, almost a loose one. According to Grahame it landed somewhere between him and the batsman. He prayed that Mead would not connect.

The batsman didn't and the fielder shot an apprehensive glance at the bowler. 'Don't worry, Mr Parker. I know what I'm doing. I've put you there for the catch.'

As he told me in retrospective amusement at the incident, Grahame Parker said: 'Nowadays I'd have the protection of three suits of armour in that position.'

Did that unreasonable demand on another fielder, I wonder, reflect a hint of sadism in the bowler's make-up? Long since, Grahame has discovered that there were direct links between the two branches of the Parker family in the mid-eighteenth century. Was that the way to treat a distant relative, Charlie?

I can only report that the short-leg theory was a source of good humour back in the dressing room. 'Any close fielder's safe when I'm bowling,' pronounced Prestbury's elder statesman.

His word was law in the dressing room and his well-spaced jokes earned a generous response. It would have been unthinkable to him that he ever lacked a sense of humour. 'Only two serious weaknesses with our team,' he and his colleagues used conversationally to trot out on convivial occasions. 'Brewers' asthma and financial cramp!' And then he was apt to offer this caustic post-script: 'Apart from that, we ain't bloody good enough.'

Parker himself generated humour: he had, after all, a face as lugubrious as Buster Keaton or Hancock. Few comedians have funny faces. Parker's infernally flapping sleeves were funny to all but the batsmen who felt they were taking on the full sails of the Spanish Armada. The players told apocryphal stories about him by the dozen – behind his back. Their favourite was a true one and has not, as far as I know, ever been made public.

An amateur called Norman Hobbs came in for half a dozen games in 1924 and ended with an average of 5.89 runs. His cricket was undistinguished; his appearance was the opposite. In every way he was splendidly attired. He even insisted on wearing a bowler hat on the way to the ground. When it came to Hobbs's first away match, the pros decided an initiation ceremony might be in order. They crouched on a balcony above the hotel entrance. And after a hissed 'Here he comes,' they emptied a large bowl of water over the man who stepped out of the hotel into the driveway. He was drenched. And it was not the immaculately dressed Hobbs at all. It was Charlie Parker.

He was not amused. Realizing in horror the extent of their mistake, the players evaporated from the balcony. 'Everyone wanted to lock himself in his bedroom,' I was told. Parker didn't forgive easily their appalling case of mistaken identity. He was especially scathing about the standard of Gloucestershire's fielding over the next week.

The irony was that he, most of all, had precious little time for many of the amateurs, with their flamboyant wardrobes and what he saw as toffee accents. His class complex was a considerable one and it distorted, I have no doubt, some of his judgments. It's true that he simply articulated, better than many of his fellow professionals, the anachronistic absurdities of the county game. His kind of socialism wasn't the intellectual prattling that you got from well-heeled coteries who either salved their consciences by throwing the names of Lenin and Marx into every coffee-sipping conversation, or found it academically fashionable, even exciting, to do so. Nor did he need to join the Fabians. His was gut radicalism: and that had no place for barriers between the amateurs and the professionals. After a tiring day in the field, during which eleven players had pooled their skills in an attempt to dismiss the opposition, it seemed unthinkable to him that the cricketers should walk off by separate gates and move to separate dressing rooms according to the school they once attended.

The result was that he sometimes bristled unnecessarily and this looked very much like a form of discourtesy.

'Why do you rub 'em all up the wrong way?' a Gloucestershire pro once asked him, discussing Parker's brittle relationship with a great many of the amateurs.

'Because of their privileged backgrounds. What do those buggers know about life?'

Such an aggressive philosophy was both a strength and weakness. His antagonism to the amateurs was not absolute. Basil Allen, a martinet of the old school, wasn't his kind of captain. Bev Lyon was. Lyon and Parker got on famously, oblivious of any social division. They played golf together, they drank together. After a win – or even a failure – Bev, ebullient as ever, would charge into the professionals' dressing room. 'Right, lads, EVERYBODY'S coming . . . The drinks are on me.'

It wasn't a matter of an unctuous amateur ingratiating himself with the pros. That wasn't the Lyon style. He genuinely liked people, whatever their backgrounds. His main cricketing aggression came when he was facing a Somerset eleven led by brother 'Dar'. I have no reason to revise a much earlier judgment that he was the most inventive and experimental captain Gloucestershire ever had. He hated a drawn match. He lived dangerously on the field. In 1931, after two days of the match with Yorkshire at Sheffield had been lost through rain, he put what in those days was an outrageous proposition to the Yorkshire captain Frank Greenwood. They both declared after scoring four byes – and Gloucestershire went on to win the match.

He didn't give a toss for the game's establishment and, with an engaging flourish – and eye to a headline – enjoyed ruffling feathers. Most of his ideas were well ahead of their time. In 1930, during a speech in Bristol, which after all used to be known as the City of Churches, he staggered his audience by coming out with an unequivocal advocacy of Sunday cricket. It was intrepid stuff at a gathering sprinkled with clerics.

Parker read the headline and loved it – for its sheer audacity. At the county club's annual dinner in 1932, the year after the contrived result at Sheffield, Lyon was fearlessly sounding off once again. I quote verbatim from part of his speech:

You've got to attract present-day crowds of young men and women who spend their shillings watching dirt-track riders risking their lives, or greyhounds hurtling round bends, or gangster films by the hundred.

There are certain highly respected and very eminent gentlemen who do not understand that changes have come about in the last fifty years. Why should they? Would Bach, Beethoven and Chopin understand Jack Payne? The policy of staying still and waiting like Mr Micawber for something to turn up seems to me to lack courage and practicality. The spacious times of the Edwardian era are gone for ever.

Lord Hawke can afford to be haughty – cricket can't. Lord Hawke fiddles while Rome burns. I'm not content to stand by while the game I love dies an unnatural death from lack of support. There is clearly one thing to do – the clock must come into the game more often. Allow batting sides only three hours in which to get their runs, and I challenge anyone to tell me how first-class cricket has been spoilt.

Why can't we have knock-out cricket, the final to be played at Lord's or the Oval? And I should like to see the profits divided equally among the counties who take part.

The incredible thing is that Bev Lyon made that speech more than half a century ago. Most of the audience applauded politely and dismissed it with an indulgent smile as 'another of Beverley's pipe dreams'. How were they to realize that he alone had the vision to see how the game had to go if it were to survive?

As a captain, Bev Lyon made mistakes and miscalculations. He never failed to keep the match alive. His approach could be as rakish as the angle of his familiar trilby in the morning as he walked briskly from the visiting team's hotel to the ground. He was a marvellous psychologist and always knew the time to pay the compliment. Andy Wilson puts it neatly. 'Bev treated Charlie as the star. He'd tell him that the team didn't have much chance but that Charlie was the only one who'd be able to do anything at all. If he didn't bowl, well they might as well pack up and go home.' Parker responded to that kind of flattery. Another pre-war professional said: 'Bev treated Charlie as both a prima donna and a genius because that was exactly what he was.'

He also treated Parker as an equal. It wasn't a fashionable notion at the time. For his part, the great bowler reckoned he was the equal of most of the amateurs. His unceasing intention was to give the pros more status and self-respect. He campaigned in his pragmatic way to introduce salary cheques for the Gloucestershire players, and to ensure a fairer deal for those who weren't in the team. 'Dignity of labour' was a phrase he'd acquired.

Once he found himself on a private tour to South Africa. He and that fine Leicestershire workhorse George Geary were heavily outnumbered by more elevated members of society. It looked as though he and George had been included to take the wickets and do the hard labour. When he stepped on board the ship, Parker went to the purser's office and asked to see the register. Perhaps he didn't know who else was going on this particular tour.

It was an imposing cricketing complement. Some of the names carried an aristocratic swagger. There were a few high-ranking military members. Initials were plentiful. That was until it came to . . . Parker C and Geary G.

All Charlie's repressed political rhetoric zoomed to the surface. He addressed the purser personally. In the course of his tirade, he said: 'You'll alter that. I want my full initials. And I want a 'Mr' put in front of it. And so does George here.'

I understand he had his way. He wasn't being arrogant for the sake of it. He was being abrasive because a social injustice, as he saw it, had made him very angry. He was having his say on behalf of all professional cricketers.

Looking back on incidents, like the physical fury in a

hotel lift, Cheltenham barside or that purser's office, it is easy to conclude at this distance that there was too much hate in Parker's heart. That wasn't really true at all. He was a terror on the field and a kindly lamb when surrounded by fellow West Country voices in the dressing room. He warmed to uncomplicated human beings like Alf Dipper ('Old Dip') and quiet little Harry Smith, the wicket-keeper. It isn't absolutely certain how much the personal regard for Harry was returned. The stumper's benefit match was at the old Packer's ground in Bristol and the weather was miserable. Everyone agreed it wasn't really fit to play but the large crowd was beginning to get restive. Reluctantly it was decided to make a start.

For an account of what happened I return to Parker's mate, Reg Sinfield. 'I've never laughed so much in my life. Charlie opened from the pavilion end. The surface was slippery as he ran up for the first delivery. He lost his footing and went ass over head. We did our best to suppress our guffaws. As for Parker, he snatched his sweater and made it clear he wasn't "bloody well going to stay out there any longer". He walked off and the rest of the team followed.'

The friendship between Parker and Sinfield must have been evident from these pages. Parker helped to bring Sinfield to Gloucestershire after a chance word on the balcony at Lord's. Reg had just been left out of the Hertfordshire side for a reason he found hard to fathom. They became dressing-room and drinking pals. Reg was a gentle soul without any of Charlie's brashness of language. He'd been on C. B. Fry's nautical training ship, the *Mercury*, and had been a champion boxer in the navy. I shall always remember him as the first Gloucestershire pro to perform the double. He scored 15,561 runs and took 1,165 wickets for the county. Like Parker, he played just once for England; like Parker, he coached schoolboys – in his case, at Clifton and Colston's – with patience and paternal talent. As I write these words, he is still doing so – well into his eighties.

Sinfield was an off-spinner and a dedicated one. Parker admired that quality. 'I kept a diagram, reminding me of the favourite shots of all the best players. When we were playing Hampshire, I astonished Bev Lyon by asking for three short legs, mostly backward. I knew that Phil Mead liked to tickle one round the corner to get off the mark. Before the game I'd joked with the umpire, Tiger Smith, that I'd catch him out one of these days. In I came to Phil. He'd seen the line of short legs and I knew that it worried him. He couldn't make up his mind what to do with the first ball. And I had him plumb lbw. But Tiger turned me down. Phil continued to look anxious, pondering about how he could get off the mark. The second ball should have been a catch behind the wicket and Harry Smith of all people put it down. With my third ball, Phil Mead snicked again and Harry held on to the ball. Tiger looked at me and said "Not many people get a hat-trick against anyone as sound as Phil." I can still see the batsman now, peering at those short legs and then pulling on that cap of his.'

There was a great mutual loyalty in the case of Parker and Sinfield. Parker believed and went to pains to insist that Wilfred Rhodes was a better bowler. His admiration for the ageless Yorkshireman was immense. Sinfield was in no doubt at all of Parker's superiority and he will still argue it with the same passion. If he was swayed a little by personal friendship, it added only interest to an absorbing comparison between two great and in some ways similar bowlers.

Parker's demonstration of loyalty to Sinfield was rather more theatrical. It emanated from the Somerset-Gloucestershire match at Taunton in 1930: M. D. Lyon versus B. H. Lyon. Brotherly love was singularly absent, even more so when Tom Goddard at mid-off put down the Somerset skipper on two. He went on to score 210.

The Jewishness of the Lyon brothers was part of their appeal. They wore their emotions for all to see. Their tongues carried charm and, when they felt it necessary, a cutting edge. Contemporaries claimed that the gifted siblings could fight 'like cat and dog'. Proud blood coursed through their veins and the rivalry was often intense.

During that particular Taunton match, Dar Lyon's double century gave him far more than a nose start over Bev. There was a justifiable swagger. The Somerset farmers shared the joke. And Bev, mostly blessed with a felicitous sense of fun, was for once not amused.

As Sinfield buckled on the pads, he asked: 'What are the tactics, skipper?'

'Put on your long spikes, Reg. Go out there and wear the wicket out.'

The ex-sailor and C. B. Fry trainee had long learned the value of obeying an order. He found himself scoring a couple of early, reluctant fours off Jack White and then nailed his bat to the crease. The maidens mounted as Sinfield moved into permanent residence. A Quantock voice from a boundary bench bellowed: 'Wos call this? It ain't cricket, mate.'

The batsman looked in the direction of his critic. He shouted back: 'But I'm still there, mate.' The taut atmosphere was eased by the collective chuckle around the ground. Everyone seemed to grasp that Sinfield was playing under orders.

He turned to the umpire. 'Sorry about this. But I'm here till half past six. I know what I've got to do.'

The innings was one of drab, undeviating efficiency. Sinfield gave no chances and scored a century. The applause, when it came, was grudging and indeed carried about as much genuine affection as a rough-and-ready Sedgemoor slaughterman would have had in those days for his sentenced beasts. Signs of mutual frigidity weren't uncommon in the Somerset-Gloucestershire games between the wars.

Back in the pavilion, Bev Lyon put his arm round the weary, obdurate batsman. 'Well done. A fine knock. You did exactly what I wanted from you.'

Parker's first comment, accompanied by one of his

wrinkled smiles, was based on pragmatism. 'Great job you done here, Reg. Roughed the wicket up nicely.'

They were prophetic words as Sinfield later discovered himself, bowling round the wicket. Somerset rather went to pieces, dissipating all the obvious advances of Dar Lyon's biggest score in championship cricket. Gloucestershire won by nine wickets. The verbal exchange between the brothers is probably unprintable.

But there is another thread to the drama, involving Parker and reflecting once more his loyalty to a friend.

It concerns the morning after Sinfield's long, laborious and unpopular innings. No one quite knew how the match was going to go; there was, however, absolutely no ambiguity about Gloucestershire's rating in the Somerset town. It was at zero-level.

As usual Parker was late getting up. He refused to hurry in the morning. Reg, with all that naval training behind him, was more obsessed with punctuality. 'Stop panickin'. We'll be at the ground on time. But I'm goin' to get me hair cut first.' That was that. Parker finished his breakfast and set off at a nine o'clock saunter for the barber's. Sinfield brought up the rear.

Charlie took his seat and asked for a haircut and shave. The barber didn't recognize either of his early-morning customers. He soon broached the subject of cricket.

'Been to the match, sir?'

Parker sniffed, half amused, wondering what was coming. 'Yes.'

'See that bloody Sinfield bloke? Never seen nothing like it. Disgrace, that's what I do call it.'

It was too good to stop in mid-flow. Parker, his face covered in lather, grunted in a non-committal way and encouraged a continuation of the monologue. 'I'll tell you what,' went on the barber, 'I'd cut his bloody throat, if he came in here.'

At the time he was brandishing his cut-throat with a reckless abandon that gave credence to the threat of homicide.

It was by now too much for Parker. He jumped to his feet, wiping the shaving soap from his mouth. 'Listen. I'm Charlie Parker. And this is me mate, Reg Sinfield.' He administered an immediate and succinct lecture on the inadvisability of small-town Sweeney Todds expressing opinions on subjects they knew nothing about.

Charlie, for all his quirks and his dogmatic approach to the argument in hand, was a staunch ally. He liked another Charlie, young Barnett, who got his first chance for Gloucestershire as a sixteen-year-old in 1927. He liked the tendency for hundreds before lunch. Parker, the perceptive batting tutor, could see what the impetuous Barnett was inclined to do wrong. 'But you'll play for England,' he said, just a little wary of this self-possessed young man educated at Wycliffe, like his father, another Gloucestershire Charles Barnett before him. Parker approved of the way father encouraged son to turn pro. There were to be twenty Tests, of course, and an indecent number of boundaries before lunch.

My mention of Barnett prompts me to return to Hammond. Gerald Howat's biography of Wally was published in 1984 and I read a particularly frank review in the *Gloucestershire and Avon Life,* a county glossy, by Charlie Barnett. He was always a man to speak assertively, without too much fear or favour; in the dressing room some of the other professionals used to call him 'The Guv'. He took a perceptive view of life from both sides of the park: as the public schoolboy and the prewar pro, later as a Cirencester fishmonger and a pink-coated country gent who rode to hounds with the Berkeley. His review of the Hammond book, written with intimate inside knowledge, was surprising for its vigour and the implication that the pair's relationship was less than cordial. The relevant passage, in the context of my study of Charlie Parker, has to do with captaincy.

'The Howat book', says Barnett, 'claims that Hammond's captaincy was a success but what I do know was that it didn't make for a happy team. We were certainly glad enough when he finished and we reverted to Basil Allen. I think his weakness was that he wasn't prepared to ask advice from others. He gave orders and woe betide if they were not carried out ... he never forgave me for questioning his authority. All I know is that it was a great deal more fun playing under the genuine amateur captains. . .'

We all know that the Hammond personality changed drastically during the time he was with Gloucestershire. The carefree, boyish, even gregarious young man who ran down the wing for the Rovers in Bristol and confided with roguish delight to his attentive fellow cricketers about what happened on his afternoons out at Weston with the girls from the local theatres, gave way to a sullen, withdrawn and snobbishly distant colleague. That sad metamorphosis isn't new.

But it now emerges that he wanted the county captaincy during the years that Bev Lyon was in charge. I have discovered that during a match at Horsham, when Lyon was absent because of his business ties, Hammond asked Parker, Goddard and Sinfield if he could have a private chat with them at the end of play.

He came straight to the point. 'None of us really want Lyon, do we? He only plays when it suits him. He goes off whenever he likes.' The other three players, all admirers of Lyon, were stunned. Hammond went on to suggest that they should approach the committee and say that the present arrangement wasn't satisfactory. Machiavellian coups aren't unknown in county cricket, of course. Scheming, disgruntled pros have been able to unseat their skipper in the Grand Manner.

But, at that Horsham meeting, Parker saw the danger and the hidden meaning in the approach. 'You want the bloody captaincy yourself, don't you Wally?' Hammond spluttered a denial. His colleagues weren't convinced.

Parker remained suspicious of Hammond. Perhaps he always considered that Wally was too close to Plum Warner for Charlie's comfort – and Test selection pros-

pects. Perhaps he felt that Hammond was loath to advo-
cate the bowler's claims at the highest level.

As a sort of paranoia seemed to grip Parker whenever
Warner was mentioned in conversation, civilized or
otherwise, it is right 'hat we should for a moment
distance ourselves from the prickly subject and analyse
why Hammond held Warner in such warm regard. It
goes deeper than the generous compliments that Plum
paid the great England player at public dinners and in
print.

Warner showed great kindness to Hammond. The
young cricketer was back from the West Indies in 1926
and gravely ill in a private Bristol hospital. There has
been much conjecture over the form of the illness. 'Plum
Warner came to see me and has said since that I was
in the valley of the shadow of death. He is a man of the
most steadfast courage who himself at that time had
only just had a "kill or cure" operation after thirty years
of continuous pain. It is absolutely true to say that his
visits put new heart into me, and perhaps provided me
with just sufficient strength to turn the dark corner. He
would not hear complaints but reassured me with such
utter confidence that I should get better and make many
hundreds for England against Australia and other
opponents that in the end I was given courage and
resistance enough to pull through. If there is such a
thing as faith healing in this world, I can recommend
with all my heart Dr. Warner.'

Those words come from Hammond's *Cricket My
Destiny*. They provide a revealing insight into the
character, frequently misunderstood, of Pelham Warner.
In some ways they were two cold men. But Hammond
was touched by such unexpected interest in his health
and well-being. The friendship was sustained and that
rankled with Parker.

On the field, of course, Parker and Hammond prowled
and pounced: as ruthless a pair of predators as the game
possessed. They were telepathic and interdependent.
Charlie imparted his wizardry, the worn ball deviating

away from leg to off. Wally was stretching forward from slip or gully. It was a superb, almost unparalleled partnership. There was never a bowler more cunning or a slip with sharper reflexes. Batsmen knew what was going to happen – and still couldn't avoid the corny capitulation. The coup de grâce was breathtakingly simple.

In *Cricketers of My Time*, A. A. Thomson wrote: 'When Hammond caught eight Surrey batsmen in one match in 1928 and eight Worcestershire men four years later, he and Parker between them had exerted a kind of mesmerism which was nearly irresistible . . . Just as the combination between Verity and Mitchell was a conspiracy, so Parker's bowling and Hammond's fielding formed a dark intrigue.'

Parker may have been a trifle indolent when it came to farm work as a boy or when pretending to look for a remunerative winter's job. But the mind was active and alert. His approach to cricket, whatever the brimstone and rustic oaths, was that of the academic. He rhapsodized, in his own unadorned way, about the skills of Rhodes and Larwood. There was no envy in his voice: he could be a man with a generous heart. He worried about what he saw were his own shortcomings. He was never quite at his best against left-handers. Frank Woolley once got a particularly effortless hundred against Parker who pondered over it for weeks. Horace Dales of Middlesex, George Brown of Hampshire, and Charles Hallows of Lancashire, all seemed to play him with relative ease.

He rebuked team mates when he knew they were devaluing their talents by a lazy stroke or a dropped catch. He never ceased to learn himself. At the age of fifty-one, during the pre-season nets, he ignored his lunch and went on for three hours because he feared he had lost 'his flighty one'.

His dedication was that of a boy hoping to break into the game. 'Where am I going wrong, Reg? Can you spot it?'

And eventually at two o'clock, Sinfield, his tummy

rumbling, did spot it. Charlie was bringing his arm too far over. He went back to the nets in the afternoon. 'I've got it back,' he said with real joy. 'Me flighty one's returned.'

Parker was late establishing himself in first-class cricket: and then came the war. He was nearly forty by the time he had made his spunky ultimatum and been accepted as a spinner. The bronzed, unsmiling face was more creased than ever in 1935 when he took 108 wickets. He was fifty-two.

The more I have researched his feats and eavesdropped on the reminiscences of his surviving contemporaries, the greater has become my admiration and respect for his sheer skills. Much of his naked aggression and spontaneous belligerence have appeared, half a century or so on, unattractive and even unforgivable. But we must evaluate him against a background of privilege, irksome social disparities and the unmistakable rustle of political change.

In 1926, when he'd already viewed the soup kitchens in Bristol's Old Market, he was invited with some more of the Gloucestershire players to take part in a match in the Forest of Dean. There were many hungry faces in that functional corner of the county, across the other side of the Severn. The host was a local coalowner and after the cricket was over he was unwise enough to make a disparaging comment about the miners of the nation. Parker sprung to his feet and unleashed the kind of tirade that stunned everyone present. The coalowner fidgeted and wished he'd never organized the match. But many, including those from local mining stock, knew Parker was right.

For someone who systematically chose to educate himself after leaving school, Parker was a man of justice, of sagacity and breadth of knowledge. He could quote the Bible, occasionally the classics – as Grahame Parker will verify – and whistle the best symphony music. Once at Trent Bridge, at the end of the day's play, he said to

74

Sinfield: 'Come on, Reg, some professor of music has invited us out for the evening.'

And so he had. Reg sat silent, inhibited by the range of the esoteric conversation. Then he became increasingly uncomfortable as Parker began to question the music expert's judgment.

As the two cricketers walked back to their digs, Sinfield turned to his intrepid companion. 'You shouldn't have done that, you know.'

Parker's reply was typically brusque. 'The old fool just didn't know what he was talking about.' That incident summed up the strength and the weakness of the man.

He died at Cranleigh on 11 July 1959. It was an irony that the local paper at Cheltenham, *The Echo*, which had always charted his mighty deeds so affectionately, was on strike and could offer no more at the time than a token mention of the death in an improvised news-sheet. The obituaries in *The Times* and *Wisden* dealt at fitting length with his prodigious talents.

Gloucestershire had great cricketers like Grace, Jessop and Hammond: and C. W. L. Parker has every right to be bracketed with them. He could bowl better than the other three – and could cuss a hundred times better.

Part Two
Parkin, Cecil Henry
(1886–1943)

Born Egglescliffe, Durham, son of railwayman
and later station master. Played for Yorkshire
(one senior appearance only, 1906) and
Lancashire 1914–26. Also played great deal of
League cricket, before, during and after his
county career. Pace-bowler-turned-off-spinner
(with many variations). Took 901 wickets.
Ten Test appearances, nine of them against
Australia in 1920 and 1921.

'I shall remember him as the greatest sticky wicket bowler of my era in first-class cricket and I feel sorry that I should have been responsible in any way for the close of his Test career'.

Arthur Gilligan

1

Only Yards Away from Yorkshire

It is one of the ironies of our first-class game that the seventh Lord Hawke, who in his way tried so hard to give the professionals of his day an improved status, was held up to such scorn. One stray, ill-chosen sentence of his, in which he rhetorically prayed to God that no professional would ever captain England, looked haughty and insensitive in print, and summoned up bitter emotions from the less privileged.

There was, of course, paternalism in his make-up. That was part of the social tableau of the times: of the man, his station and the ingrained attitudes of those who accepted that the Almighty had ordained rigid dividing lines, and that only a relative few would dress for dinner.

Lord Hawke, who died in 1938, remains one of the mighty influences on our domestic game. He was President and later Treasurer of the MCC and for a decade at the turn of the century was an England selector. His voice, when it came to cricket's administration, was clear, authoritative and unequivocal. His contemporaries said he could be intimidating; but his words carried sound reason and at times, despite his reputation, compassion.

As a cricketer he captained Yorkshire for twenty-eight years, although his birth certificate betrayed native allegiance to Lincolnshire. He had a pleasant cover drive, scored thirteen centuries altogether and played five times for England. His Test record was undistinguished and it isn't unreasonable to conclude that the selectors were given an eye-winking aristocratic prod. But as a captain of Yorkshire he was worth his place as a player. Eight times under his leadership the county won the championship.

His relationship with the game's professionals was a fascinating one, and that will lead us on to Cecil Parkin. He believed in the social order of the day. His accent and bearing were many a mile and many a decanter of port removed from the flat, functional vowels and the shuffling deportment he saw around him in the side streets of Bradford, Leeds and Sheffield. In conversation with many of the bewhiskered amateurs he could be dismissively condescending about the little knots of gauche, raw-grained pros who acknowledged the demands of separatism and earned for themselves a mean and disproportionate amount of net practice. Yet Lord Hawke also extended to them a degree of affection that was rare and, at committee level, unpopular.

He would take a professional aside and say to him: 'You are drinking your wages away'. Maybe he was more concerned with athletic well-being in the outfield. But it horrified him that so many of the pros of his day would come off the field, wipe the sweat off their faces and then hand over what remained of their weekly pittance to the nearest landlord. He never understood the pitiful philosophy of the working classes to snatch at the elusive bonhomie to be found in the stone-floored bars, and to allow the alcoholic fumes to glaze over the futility of hand-to-mouth existence.

Lord Hawke, rather like a well-intentioned house master, gave the pros a pep talk. He introduced winter pay for them. He smartened them up and told them, in kindly if feudal tones, that they were representing their county all the time. His meticulous regard for discipline didn't please all of them. One or two with a streak of rebellion dared to question the club rules he imposed.

His fury descended on them. They were soon packing their bags for good.

For every valid reason, many of the amateurs were disliked by those who were nominally paid to play. The amateurs were inclined to get into the county sides by nepotism, country-house favours and connections that were more masonic than sporting in spirit. But the Yorkshire pros mostly came to like Hawke. He could bluster and keep them in their place; yet they discovered he had a good heart. He showed them how to invest their benefit money. Long after he, and they, had given up playing and he was president of the county – a position he held till his death – they would exchange warm words and memories at the club's annual meetings. The pros were less frightened of him by then.

He liked Cec Parkin less. They had first met when Parkin was on the point of joining Yorkshire and there had been a problem over geographical qualification. Lord Hawke noted with some alarm the self-confidence of the Durham lad. He didn't approve of professionals who had too much to say for themselves. It wasn't good for the status quo – or the liver.

The interview, conducted at the Yorkshire ground, could have been an inhibiting one for the unworldly Parkin. The two of them sat together, across a polished table. Lord Hawke was an important figure and Parkin knew all about the reputation. 'We're having a few silly objections, Parkin, about where you were born. I've been checking with Mr Charles Townsend and Mr Wreford Brown, and it seems you are very nearly a Yorkshireman.'

'Aye, that's right, sir. Just over other side of t'border. Only matter of few yards.'

Lord Hawke contemplated the proximity of native belonging. 'Yes, well Parkin. A few yards, you say. Who's worried about a few yards. You play today.'

It was maybe the momentary cunning of the Lincoln poacher. There were a few meaningless pleasantries and some chirpy responses from this almost unknown league

81

cricketer. Busines was done. 'Thank you, Parkin. I hope you have a good game.' He waved vaguely in the direction of the door. Later he was to say to another senior committee member: 'That fellow Parkin is very sure of himself, I must say.' It is unlikely the president was consumed with regret when the player's registration was found to be invalid. Parkin moved on to Lancashire instead.

Lord Hawke, we can assume, never took too kindly to him. He was later to be publicly generous when it came to praising the off-spinner. He applauded the Test recognition, observed the mounting statistic of wickets and must have wished more than once that Parkin's mother had shifted the location of her confinement by a boundary length or two.

What the Yorkshire president did not like – and said so with bristling indignation – was Cecil's propensity for trenchant views about the game. He expressed them at will, often with an engaging smile to soften the calculated dig. Such observations, about the state of the game and, more provocatively, about specific individuals, were made in the dressing room or at the bar. They also gained a far wider currency when they appeared in the newspapers.

Cec Parkin, like many a North Countryman, was blunt and fearless. He hadn't too much time for diplomatic niceties, of the kind you are apt to associate with a pussy-footing southerner. Sports writers in the 1920s quickly detected that he had an undeniable flair for a contentious phrase. He was never unduly reticent when approached for an opinion, at least not until his relationship with journalists had soured and he had started to walk reluctantly away from a headline.

In the 1920s, the style of the sports pages was changing. Circulation battles were gaining momentum and 'signed' articles by leading sportsmen were proving a notable attraction. The reading public was gullible and had never heard of such an emergent breed as ghost-writers. Parkin was able to supplement his cricket wages

82

with regular postal orders from the papers. His views were avidly read, on a weekly basis, in the old *Empire News*. And those views, at the behest of the wily sports editor, invariably had a sting to them. Poor Lord Hawke was wont to splutter over his Sunday breakfast. For heaven's sake, what right had this nominally educated professional to opinionate on major cricketing issues?

The Parkin remarks directed against his England captain Arthur Gilligan were bad enough and in 'appalling taste', according to Hawke. They were sensational in any context, and the cruel turning point of the player's career. We shall be returning to them inevitably in greater detail.

The repercussions to that unprecedented criticism by a Test cricketer of his skipper were voluminous and acrimonious. For the moment, one should not pre-judge. It was a strange affair and maybe it is time to examine again the explanation of Parkin and those who knew him best, including his son Reginald. But it must be said that the backlash of anger to his reported attitude to Gilligan as a tactician and especially as a handler of bowlers didn't dissuade him from more published controversy.

In one of his articles he was even audacious enough to suggest that England might do worse than appoint a professional captain. Surely Parkin had few equals as a polemicist. He couldn't have said or written anything more likely to arouse the collective wrath of the establishment. He was daring to speak the unspoken. London clubs were suddenly alive with talk of horse-whipping vengeance as heavy-eyed old colonels stumbled from their leather-bound somnolence.

' What's wrong with Herbert Sutcliffe or Jack Hobbs?' he asked with, one suspects, more mischief than naïvete.

This was too much for Lord Hawke. And at the next annual meeting of Yorkshire County Cricket Club he thundered out his protest. It was unfortunate for him that the public remembered only one fervent sentence: 'Pray God no professional will ever captain England.' As a schoolboy nurtured on cricketing rather than historical data, I could quote it more often – and certainly more accurately – than Nelson's valedictory murmur to Hardy.

His Lordship said a good deal more in that impassioned speech. He assured the Yorkshire members, for instance, that he loved professionals 'every one of them'. That must have been an excessive claim and would certainly have been disputed by the two pros he dismissed for good from the Yorkshire dressing room, one, we all know, for imbibing too zestfully and then peeing on the field. But there was ample evidence of his affection for the humbler members of the county team. What he wanted to say was that England had always had an amateur captain and it would be a great pity if things changed. In retrospect, we may see him as a blinkered aristocrat but his fashionable defence of the amateur skipper was utterly sincere. His speech won prolonged applause. Cecil Parkin was again cast as the villain.

Parkin, the happy-go-lucky jester, discovered for a second time just how unpopular he had become. At home, he buried his head in his hands and turned to his wife: 'I feel unwanted for no just reason. I think I'll chuck county cricket altogether. There's no joy in being cold-shouldered.'

He was more depressed and miserable than at any other time in his life. When he was told that Hawke had said: 'If he was still a Yorkshire player, I'd make sure he'd never step onto a Yorkshire cricket field again,' Parkin wished with all his heart that he was still back in Norton-on-Tees, working as an apprentice pattern maker.

The gregarious off-spinner sensed that he was being shunned. For several years he had been one of this country's most popular cricketers. His wicket-taking feats for Lancashire were beginning to fill the record books. He was the BOWLER people came to watch. They were entranced by the sheer variety of his deliveries; they were entertained by the discomfiture of the batsmen who sparred at him and pondered his cheeky spectrum of challenge. And, on top of all that, he was one of nature's jokers. Cricket could always be fun when he was around: palming the ball like the magician he was, under the nose of a gawping umpire, hiding it in his pocket, kicking it up into his hand with his right boot in a way all the kids tried to copy. Yet here he was, because of published views that were before their time, being maligned and ostracized.

He said: 'The result of all this hubbub is that I have been made to appear very small. There seems no end to the stir, caused first by the Gilligan and then the Lord Hawke incident. The memory of them is engraved on my brain. They have spoilt my career in first-class cricket, which has been one of such pleasure up to now.'

In his published memoirs, *Cricket Triumphs and Troubles*, he had this to say of the Hawke retort to his intrepid suggestion that a professional captain might usefully be considered:

There was a rare rumpus. I was attacked in the press and out of it . . . They were quickly after me for more interviews but I declined all their invitations and did not say another word on the subject. . . All along I felt I was grossly misunderstood in the whole affair and that what I meant to be a perfectly innocent and fair comment was acting like a boomerang and hitting me. I want to say now, as I have so often stated in my published writings, that no one has a greater admiration for amateur skippers than I have. And no one has been more content to play under their leadership. But amateur skippers should be capable of holding their positions on their merits as players. I still say that if such men were not forthcoming, England should choose a professional as captain. I was surprised Lord Hawke adopted the attitude he did. There was no cause for offence.

From this distance, none of us would say that Cecil

Parkin's bold suggestion was irrational. It was the kind of thing the pros were saying more and more – but mostly from the privacy of their own poky dressing room. The idea that Sutcliffe might eventually lead Yorkshire had even been discreetly ventilated. Parkin's crime was that, for the first time, he had said aloud the things that others only whispered. He had also said them with a sweeping lack of subtlety, but that was the style of the man.

'Not everyone agrees with Lord Hawke,' he told his intimates. He was especially pleased when he read that the Governor General of Australia, Lord Forster, said at an official cricket luncheon that he wouldn't hesitate to play under Jack Hobbs. 'I was comforted by the remarks of a gentleman of such high standing as the former Kent captain, and was more grateful to him than he will ever know.'

But, of course, the days of Vic Wilson and Brian Close, the early professional skippers of Yorkshire, were still rather a long way off. There was a war to come in the meantime.

2

Wifely Devotion –
in the Art of Spin

Cecil's father was proud of the fact that he worked on the railways. At Yarm-on-Tees in Durham, near where 'young Ciss' was born at Egglescliffe, he'd stand outside the George and Dragon and point to the plaque. 'Look at that, lad. Here in 1820 they held the promoters' meeting of the Stockton and Darlington Railway. First public railway in the world, lad.' The viaduct which carried the lines over the Tees for half a mile still dominates the small town of Yarm.

By the time the family moved to Norton, a good-looking village to the north of Teesside, dad was the station master and Cecil's boyish notions were in conflict. They lived on the premises. Through one window the boy would watch mesmerically as the hissing rolling stock lumbered to and fro, smudging the panes that were cleaned with such care each day. Through another window he gazed with just as much romantic wonder at the Norton-on-Tees cricket ground. It ran almost up to the quaint little booking office.

Young Parkin was slim and fit. Every dry day he ran on to the field, tennis ball in hand. He pretended he could hit sixes right up to the railway lines, like the grown-ups did on Saturday afternoons. Every time a loco went by he tingled with excitement. But cricket was winning by the hour.

Norton took its cricket very seriously. There were

famous sportsmen who came to watch or serve on the committee. They liked Cecil's enthusiasm and put him in the first team when he was twelve. He never bowled, seldom at No 11 had the chance of an innings but chased everything like a hare in the outfield. Such youthful zest is an invaluable asset in village cricket, especially when the team has an engaging geriatric quality.

On the boundary bench which he reached late in the day straight from the office, on those weekends when he couldn't play, Charles Townsend nodded with approval. So did the Norton curate, the Rev. Wreford Brown, of the famous Corinthian footballing family. The boy would come in at tea, hot and perspiring from the outer reaches of the meadowland, to listen in awe to the kindly words of advice from the club's elders. Could that really be the marvellous Townsend, pupil of 'WG', who walked straight into the Gloucestershire side as a sixteen-year-old from Clifton College? Cecil would watch trance-like at the way this tall, distinguished solicitor could turn the ball at will from the leg – or the other way if it was his whim. And the boy had never seen a better left-hand bat. So much more time to play the shot than most of the village players.

'Tell us about that hat-trick then, Mr Townsend,' they would all plead as part of the Saturday evening ritual, before he had changed and left with his friends. Parkin was seven when he read about it: about the way William Brain, also from Clifton and playing just one season for Gloucestershire, figured with Townsend in a unique stumping hat-trick. It was achieved, sweetly, against Somerset.

It always embarrassed Townsend rather. 'Yes, well, old chap. . . We were playing at Cheltenham. And the spinner always had a chance there. And, well, Bill Brain was in splendid form that day.'

Townsend actually went on playing intermittent county cricket until 1922. 'WG' was inclined to over-bowl him in the early days. When the spin receded, he concentrated with great success on his batting. Here was the man who scored 224 against Essex and played twice for England. A celebrity indeed at Norton, alongside old Mr Parkin's station.

We can only guess how many more runs he'd have scored and how many more wickets he'd have taken if he had not devoted himself to a legal career. He became the Official Receiver at Stockton-on-Tees and died there in 1958.

'I've got a lot to thank Mr Townsend for,' Cec Parkin used later to say as he journeyed back in spirit to the Norton outfield. 'And the Reverend [Wreford Brown], not least because he took my wedding service!' He also had a great regard for Harry Anthony, who had played for Nottinghamshire and went on to be Norton's professional. Young Parkin would look up at that worldly-wise face, still bronzed from summers in the sun, and privately decide that was what he too wanted to do.

Instead he found himself an apprentice pattern maker. The prospects were unspectacular and carried not half of the prestige of being the local station master. 'It's steady, Cecil. You don't want to go down the mines.' Paternal guidance was rarely far away. When to his utter surprise and joy, sixteen-year-old Parkin was invited to become the pro to North Ormesby in the North Yorkshire and South Durham League, his father solemnly shook his head. 'T'lads's too young for any of that nonsense.'

He resented the counsel. But by now he was confident enough to think he would be asked again. He practised harder than any other member of the Norton club and was turning into a capable batsman. The trouble was no one ever suggested that he might be able to bowl, too. At the age of eighteen he had a successful trial with Ossett as a batsman – and was signed as their professional for the following season.

'Can you bowl as well, son?' they asked. 'Aye, and can take a few wickets for you,' he lied. In truth, he came out top of the bowling averages, an astonishing achievement for a lad whose sole tuition in the art had come from studying Mr Townsend – from a distance. Cecil gripped the ball instinctively; he knew nothing of such esoteric matters as movement off the pitch or through the air. But he was already becoming a self-confident youngster with an extrovert tendency. He rather fancied the idea of being a fast bowler: the glamorous figure, the shirt-billowing aggressor, so often the match winner.

Off a run-up of varying length and with an action of perky optimism rather than classic refinement, Parkin took 116 wickets that first summer for Ossett. 'Fast? Aye, I was, that. Too hot for George Hirst and Harry Haley, the Yorkshire coach, when they came to have a look at me. Hey, they even changed their minds and decided not to put their pads on to face me!'

We'll never know whether the retrospective boast could be substantiated. Hirst and Haley, two astute assessors of another man's worth at cricket, hurried back to headquarters. Oblivious to the Parkin pedigree, paraded in the main to the passing steam trains at Norton – and confined to passable batting and some fine catches at long leg – the Yorkshire duo recommended that he should be given a county game.

In theory it was a preposterous idea. Did ever a bowler go into a first-class match with fewer overs behind him? Why, at Norton they hardly entrusted him to bowl in the nets. And yet we suspect that cricket, in Victorian and Edwardian days, was full of aberrations in matters of selection. A word through the heavy cigar smoke to the president, from a doting parent about a weak-chinned son just about to come down from university or back briefly from a trading post in the Empire, so frequently led to a county debut of embarrassing consequences.

Parkin found himself chosen to play for Yorkshire against Gloucestershire at Headingley in the July of 1906. There it was to be, indelibly in *Wisden*. 'We're told you're quite quick, Parkin. See what you can do against

Gloucestershire. They haven't got Mr Jessop coming up to captain them at Leeds.'

Jessop's absence had to be a matter for relief. He had an insensitive attitude towards the proven skills of established bowlers. He'd have been intent on destroying for ever any semblance of confidence from a fledgeling operator like Parkin. Long after he had retired from the game and was serving behind the bar of one of his pubs or hotels, Cecil would be asked regularly to name the greatest batsman he ever bowled against. 'I'll tell thee one thing. Gilbert Jessop was the mightiest hitter — by a mile.' And then he'd go on, between pulling the pints of North Country-brewed ale, to tell of the match at Old Trafford just before the First World War. Jessop, crouching in that characteristic way — though no one would dare mention it in his hearing (how he hated being called The Croucher) — opened for Gloucestershire. He took guard and immediately belted Harry Dean for three sixes. Soon it was Parkin's turn.

'The first ball came flashing past my nose and thudded against the sight screen. The next one was clouted into the pavilion enclosure. I saw A. H. Horner, our captain, laughing at me. . .'

It wasn't the only time he had caught team mates, amateurs and professionals, chuckling at his expense. He didn't much like it. Off the fifth ball of the over he bowled Jessop. As he walked past the bowler on his way back to the pavilion, the great batsman, so much smaller in stature than he seemed when in outrageous full flow, turned and said: 'Well bowled, boy.' He could be a taciturn man and had the rather grim exterior of the schoolmaster he once was. By his standards, the compliment to Parkin was a generous one.

The conquering bowler later wrote: 'Gilbert Jessop had scored 35 off eleven balls in seven minutes. I was very glad when he was out. I was frightened to death and felt he might hit one back and kill me!'

But Jessop was missing from the Gloucestershire team on the July day Parkin made his debut and only senior appearance for Yorkshire. There had been the business of the residential qualification but Lord Hawke and his committee cronies had agreed that no one would bother too much about a few yards.

Parkin arrived at the Leeds ground, an unfamiliar face to the gateman and most of those with whom he was to share a dressing room. He was a good-looking young man, bright-eyed and buoyant. His thick, dark hair was watered back. He looked about him and realized he was surrounded by great Yorkshire cricketers. Hirst, Rhodes and Haigh: what illustrious company, among whom he'd be expected to bowl out Gloucestershire. George Hirst was on his way that summer to the record that is unlikely ever to be beaten. He scored 2,385 runs and took 208 wickets in 1906. He could do no wrong. Wilfred Rhodes was daring, by the compounding grandeur of his figures with bat and ball, to be mentioned in the same hallowed breath as Grace. And then there was Schofield Haigh, he of the long jumper's stride, the five hat-tricks, the fast bowler's virtues as well as the gentle, engaging humour that was instantly to appeal to Parkin, himself an incorrigible comic.

The match was never finished. There was no play at all on the second day because of rain and three interruptions for bad light after that. Parkin batted at No 11 and was out for a duck, caught off George Dennett, that splendid and underrated slow left-arm bowler who on one occasion in that 1906 season went through the Essex innings on his own at Bristol. Parkin was given eight overs, during which time he conceded 23 runs and took two wickets. It was hardly a failure. The memory of his dismissals remained vividly in his mind. Frank Edgecumbe Thomas, an amateur who played on and off as a batsman over five years, was well caught by Rothery, while Henry Huggins, more generously blessed as a bowler than a batsman, was patently beaten for pace. 'Well done, old sonner,' shouted Haigh. 'You made that one whizz.' Schofield, unlike many professional cricketers who subconsciously felt threatened by even the

Cecil Parkin

Lord Hawke

They called Cec 'Bag of Tricks'

Happy times at Old Trafford.
Congratulations for Cecil Parkin
from county captain Jack Sharp

Handshakes from Parkin and Johnny Tyldesley.
Between them is that magnificent Australian
and Lancashire fast bowler Ted Macdonald

The MCC team of 1920

Lancashire County Cricket Club in 1920. Back row: H. Rylance, L. Cook, J. Hallows, R. Tyldesley, E. Tyldesley, C. Parkin, J. Tyldesley, J. S. Heap. Front row: H. Makepeace, R. H. Spooner, J. Sharp (captain), F. W. Musson, H. Dean

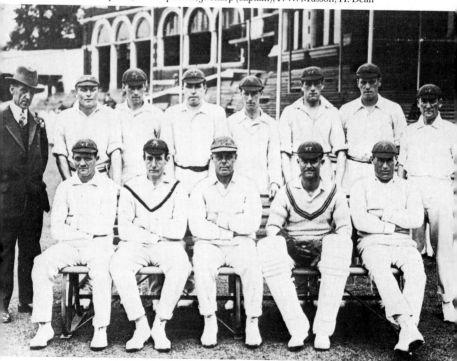

Arthur Gilligan, inevitably part of the Parkin
story (right) with Johnny Douglas

Mrs Parkin, who intrepidly helped to teach
Cec the art of spin bowling

Cecil Parkin, demonstrating the bowling action – before and after the waistline
had broadened

remotest hint of competition, was always ready to praise. Many boys at Winchester College, where he later went as coach, noticed the genuine warmth of his encouragement to others.

There were a few matches for Yorkshire's 2nd XI but then came the MCC telegram, prompted by some personal or collective complaint, that objections were being raised to the player's qualifications.

We'll never know what the young, ambitious Parkin made of this bureaucratic conflict or the fact that people had protested about where he was born.

His days with Yorkshire were clearly over. It was something of a let-down, especially after his Lordship's implication that all would be well. The transitory acquaintance with the county club hadn't been long enough for him to prove anything. He viewed the perfunctory words of praise, extended to him as he passed committee members on the stairs, as hollow sentiments. His pride had been slightly wounded; now he was going back to his pals, hoping to convince them that he was parting company with the county because of pedantic objections and red tape and not because he wasn't good enough.

It helped a little that the testimonials that followed him from Yorkshire were the kind to ensure future employment back in the league. One, from the captain of the 2nd XI, described Parkin as 'a born cricketer'. It went on: 'He's a very good man to have on your side – he is such a pleasant, cheerful fellow. Personally I am very sorry that Durham claimed him by birth.'

So the engaging facet of the player's complicated personality was already visible. He was cheerful. It was an adjective used repeatedly by friends and fellow cricketers to convey what, in the visible sense, he was like. Even at those rare times, when his standing was at its lowest because of one of those capricious attacks of his on cricket's hierarchy, the paradox of the public's reaction remained. 'Old Ciss is sounding off again but we couldn't do without him.'

R. C. Robertson-Glasgow, most humane and felici-
tously readable of cricket's essayists, wrote: 'He enjoyed
fantasy, experiment and laughter. He loved cricket from
top to toe, and he expected some fun in return.'

Fun, Cecil Parkin believed, belonged to the spinners.
He had sampled briefly the glamour of the fast bowler
and was to treasure, until the day he died, a letter from
George Hirst implying that he was very fast indeed.
Parkin was struck by the irony of it all. But how often,
he asked himself, did he see a pace bowler with a grin
on his face? They were altogether too solemn a breed.
Now spinners, those cunning exponents of finger
dexterity and legalized jiggery-pokery, were different.
They looked as though they enjoyed themselves. This
modest batsman, who turned almost by accident into an
opening pace bowler, was ready to try his luck as a
spinner.

It was more than a coincidence that Sydney Barnes,
peerless bowler and idol of league cricket in North Staffordshire, Lancashire, Bradford and Central Lancashire,
was the great hero of Parkin's life. He could turn the
ball almost as he liked at brisk medium-pace. Parkin
had watched him and envied him.

But it was more than the wizardry of those manipu-
lative fingers that the younger man admired. He knew
that Barnes was an individualist; he went his own way
in life, uninfluenced by haughty advice and the conven-
tional patterns of the professional cricketer. He played
a few token games for Warwickshire and then had two
seasons for Lancashire just after the turn of the century.
That was it: he preferred being with his native county,
Staffordshire, complemented by his league commit-
ments. It was a personalized philosophy that bewildered
many of the game's pundits. There is no point at this
distance attempting to unravel the mind and attitudes
of this bowling genius. Certainly he could be tetchy and
argumentative. He wanted the rate – and frequently,
more than the rate – for the job. He knew his value and
wasted no time over simpering self-effacement. He could

be a difficult man to handle. He clashed with Lancashire over winter employment and a benefit; he was no product of a charm school and had an abrasive edge in his dealings with club officials. No other Test player had been plucked straight from Minor Counties or league cricket. Against a thousand predictions he got on well with Archie MacLaren, who captained him and talked to him in a way he respected. 'We only ever had one row,' Barnes used to say, and that was how the field should be set to Jessop.

Parkin, of course, had a far softer character and possessed much more charm. But he marvelled at the sheer range of Barnes's bowling weaponry – and cherished the reported range of the invective. Barnes, for his part, liked Parkin and in 1910 recommended him for the pro's job at Church, the Lancashire League club. Barnes had been there before.

First, Parkin had three years in Staffordshire, playing for Tunstall. Inspired by Barnes – not to mention Bernard Bosanquet, inventor of the googly, who used to go along for the occasional game with Norton, invited by Charlie Townsend – Cecil got to work on his spinners. He was entirely self-taught.

There were hours to kill at Tunstall. Day after day, he'd go to the ground and borrow a few worn balls from the old wooden clubhouse. Then he would studiously wrap his fingers round the seam and have whole morning and afternoon sessions, until his joints hurt, trying first to turn his deliveries from the off and then from the leg. He had one loyal and uncomplaining companion, his wife.

It was a bizarre sight. She had never picked up a bat before they arrived at Tunstall and her interest in cricket was minimal. After he gave up the game, he wrote at length about the devotion of his wife. At times she was hurt when the ball spun against her thigh or her arms. 'She became my Aunt Sally. I saw her crying with pain scores of time. But she never gave up.'

I discussed this with the son, Reg, and his father's

detailed description of what took place on the almost deserted cricket ground clearly bothered him. 'I just can't bring myself to believe it. I'm sure it was exaggerated.'

Cec Parkin attributed his subsequent success as a spin bowler to the patience and the courage of his wife. 'To her I want to say the best words of gratitude that I can think of. Not only because of her help at cricket but in everything else. Our marriage has been perfectly happy all the time, even though I once gave her a black eye.' His version was that their roles were reversed and she was bowling to him when the intended return catch slipped through her protective fingers. More love hath no woman. . .

He may have acquired the fundamental skill of spin bowling but he lacked the confidence to put it into practice during any of the league matches. He stuck to medium-fast. It served him and Church CC well; each year, up to 1915, he improved on his tally of wickets and no one in the Lancashire League took more. The action had become smoother and the delivery whippier. Each summer, apart from 1914, he took well over 100 wickets. Even when he missed seven matches because of injury in 1914, he finished up with ninety-one wickets.

It was now time for Lancashire to perk up. He went along to Old Trafford to play against a strong county side in what amounted to a trial match. There were two of these and he took six wickets both times. He argued to himself that no trialist could do more to win himself a county place.

He was demoralized by the letter his league club received from Lancashire. They implied he was too thin and would therefore lack stamina. He could, in fact, in those frugal prewar days have done with a few juicy steaks. He was more than six foot tall – and weighed under nine stone. There were hundreds of working-class men, who looked just like him. That was what he used to notice about many of the amateurs: their girths reflected good living. Healthy flesh, inclined to overhang frayed school ties at waist level, did not necessarily make agile cricketers. Few of the amateurs possessed the darting brilliance of Jessop, for instance, as he vigilantly prowled the covers. The frail Parkin could still bowl for up to three hours at a stint in the Lancashire League, and then chase forty yards for a well-timed catch in the outfield. Lack of stamina? He bristled at such a superficial judgment of his physical potential.

For all sorts of ominous reasons, not much to do with a young man's ability to excel in white flannels, 1914 was an indeterminate season for county cricket. Selection was never an easy matter for Lancashire. Even though Parkin had broken his ankle and missed some of the fixtures for Church, he appeared to remain the most discussed bowler in local league cricket. 'Ee, this lad is moosterd,' knowing observers assured the county committee.

In fact, Cecil was by then no longer a lad. He was twenty-eight – with a mind of his own, even if the trait was apt to be obscured by a jokey approach to the game and an increasing inclination to play up to the spectators.

He harboured the fact that a few ageing committee members at Lancashire had let it be known they thought him too skinny for first-class cricket. When they came back with a second invitation, he prevaricated. 'The county sent an SOS to my club and asked them to release me so that I could play against Leicestershire at Liverpool. This time I wasn't so ready to jump at the opportunity. I had to be persuaded a bit.'

Not that he was completely fit. His broken ankle had not completely mended and was still giving him some pain. He didn't want to give any of those detractors the chance to confirm their irritating doubts about his ability.

Cecil Parkin's debut for Lancashire was, in fact, one of exceptional merit. The headline writers called it sensational. An unknown cricketer from the league had

become a national name on the strength of one performance. It took minds momentarily off Europe.

The Aigburth pitch was heavily saturated with rain
on the first day. Parkin gazed through the pavilion
window and suspected there were wickets ahead for him.
No one in the dressing room asked him to do a conjuring
trick or two to while away the time. They didn't in those
days know what he could do with a pack of cards.

He took fourteen wickets in that extraordinary match
and Lancashire won by eight wickets. *Wisden* observed
with some excitement: 'The outstanding feature was the
highly effective bowling of Parkin. Right hand, on the
quick side of medium, he varied his pace and pitch
with great skill and, breaking both ways, he had all the
Leicestershire batsmen in difficulties. He came out with
the splendid record of 14-99. Not often can a bowler have
made a more gratifying first appearance for a county.'

He bowled five batsmen in both the first and second
innings. It was a collector's piece, to be rightly paraded
with the game's finest debuts. The figures were: 25-8-
65-7 and 26.1-9-34-7.

One of those he bowled – and long remembered with
relish the dismissal – was C. J. B. Wood, a captain and
secretary of his county who after all scored thirty-four
centuries and nearly 24,000 runs for Leicestershire. He
was almost comically foxed by the quickish turn of one
of Parkin's best deliveries of the match. His reaction was
swift and dramatic. He swung round in a fit of pique
and in a churlish gesture knocked all three stumps out
of the ground with his bat.

Not quite the standards of sportsmanship instilled,
at least theoretically, in Cecil John Burditt Wood at
Wellingborough School, where he had shown such
promise as a cricketer that he was in the school eleven
at the age of thirteen.

We shouldn't be too severe on him. During a career
with Leicestershire that spanned twenty-seven years and
saw him play as both a professional and amateur, he
once put on 380 with Whitehead for the first wicket

against Worcestershire. The county's greybeards quote with even more basking pride the fact that at Bradford in 1911 he carried his bat through two completed innings of a first-class match. There were two typically watchful centuries by him and he was out on the field for the whole of the game. He was a fine servant of Leicestershire; behind his back a few of the pros good-naturedly called him The Coalman. Wood was a coal merchant, who loved his sport as much as his business activities. Some said he'd have been just as successful as a soccer player. As a young man he played at half back for Leicester Fosse, the forerunner of Leicester City.

Cec Parkin never forgot that flash of paddy when Wood played and missed against him in 1914. It was a story he retold with chuckles and embellishments.

In that one Liverpool match during the July of 1914 Parkin had indisputably become a county cricketer. *Wisden* enthused at the end of the season: 'A player of remarkable powers has been found. Unfortunately he could not, because of his League engagement, take part in county matches that began at the end of the week. He played in six matches for Lancashire heading the averages with thirty-four wickets for less than 16 runs each. Had he been available all through the season, Lancashire's record might have been far more worthy of the county. . .'

Just half a dozen games . . . and then the war. Parkin went to work as a fuel overseer at Oswaldtwistle. On Saturdays he played for Undercliffe in the Bradford League. There was little chance for practice and the competitive edge seemed artificial. The league cricket still offered a marvellous psychological fillip to offset personal anguish and national anxiety. C. B. Llewellyn, the South African and Hampshire player, was in the same side as Parkin; so, remarkably, was Nottingham's George Gunn.

Indeed it could be argued that the only decent cricket played during the war was in the leagues. That was where, if you were lucky, you'd find Herbert Sutcliffe,

Jack Hobbs, Frank Woolley, Syd Barnes, Schofield Haigh and Bill Hitch. What joyous riches for the soldier on leave. What acrid reminders of feats that might still have been.

Parkin nominally turned his arm over and wondered, like all the rest, whether he'd ever play county cricket again.

He did, of course, with prodigious success. By the time the war was over he was thirty-two: by any standards it was late to become a full-time county player. But by then the head was full of craft and cunning, and the fingers full of tricks. The career ahead was to prove short and, on and off the field, highly eventful.

It's a good moment to take a renewed look at The Player.

3

Conjurer On and Off the Field

Could there be a better starting point than Sir Neville Cardus? That expert and romantic eye seldom strayed too far from Lancashire in the summers when Cecil Parkin excelled for the county. His affection for the player was manifested so often in that elegant, allusive style to be seen daily in the *Manchester Guardian*. Some of the older pros hardly knew what to make of Cardus. His writing was too scholarly for them, though he'd go to pains to assure them – when they taunted him about the long words he used – that his own official education wasn't prolonged and he was proud of his many lowbrow tastes, including the music hall. Only the amateurs, for the most part, saw the *Manchester Guardian*. Its match reports were unequalled. Occasionally one of the amateurs would walk into the professionals' room before the start of play. 'Look, Ciss, Cardus has been saying some nice things about you again.' A paragraph devoted to you by Neville Cardus was regarded by many pros, including Parkin, as the consummate accolade.

In one of his essays, taken from the *Playfair Cardus,* he was to write:

And who indeed was Cecil Parkin? He was one of the greatest right hand off-breakers I have seen anywhere. And he, at his best, bowled rather above medium. In 1921 at Leeds, in the England v Australia Test, he gave

H. L. Hendry a duck first ball; and one of the stumps went flying yards.

On a turning pitch he was unplayable. I used to watch him from behind the bowler's arm. On his day I used to imagine that he was attacking any great player I had ever known – Ranjitsinghji, George Gunn, Fry, Trumper, Macartney. And I could not think of any sort of science or skill by means of which they could have survived against Parkin. He attacked, given the right sun-baked, rain-drenched turf, from round the wicket.

He exploited a leg-trap, one of the first ever to do so: three crouching fielders round the batsman's left hip and bottom. But they were not put there defensively. Parkin aimed to hit the stumps; the leg-trap catches were sent by God-'elp-me strokes, reflex action by batsmen bowled all the way, the death-spin singing in their ears. At Gravesend in 1923, after showers and sun, Parkin saw me between innings and said: 'You can cancel your hotel booking for tomorrow night.' Kent were dismissed for seventy-two and 131. Parkin took 10-58 in the match.

He didn't polish the ball on his trousers all day and depend on the workings of the seam – though, if needs be, he could take a new ball and open at the pace of Trevor Bailey, and faster. He could do everything with a cricket ball. . .

Parkin had a touch of genius. It is only mediocrity that is consistently at its best. Nobody who saw him could forget him in a lifetime. He let out sparks of personality. And you can't legislate cricketers into personalities.

Genius is a term cast carelessly about in the context of cricket. I once dared to use it about Harold Gimblett, the sad Somerset cavalier, but not because I pretended he scored runs like Bradman. My compliment emanated from my regard for the rare, moody, enchanting, elevating and inspirational style of the man.

Cardus spoke of genius when it came to Parkin. So did Rex Pogson, when he wrote so well of Lancashire in *The County Cricket Series*.

Genius is not too strong a word. Potentially, he was one of the greatest bowlers in the history of the game. He wanted to be every kind of bowler at one and the same time. He was a conjurer on the field (and a talented conjurer off the field) and the rabbits he brought out of the hat sometimes embarrassed his own side as much as his opponents.

As a fast-medium bowler Parkin was probably only inferior to Tate in the inter-war years. He had a delightful action, lively and loose-limbed, with the arm high and the follow-through full and straight. He could spin the ball at speed and bring it back sharply from outside the off stump. If he had been content to be one of the best fast-medium bowlers of his day he might have been more successful than he was, but he would not have been Parkin.

That's a bold claim, putting him so close to Tate. There are views in that striking assessment which are guaranteed to form the basis of countless winter-evening arguments. It is part of the timeless, stimulating appeal of cricket, like those 'imponderables' as we attempt to compare great players from different eras.

Because he was such a perceptive judge of cricketers, nestling his opinions without any hint of pomposity in that happy style of his, Robertson-Glasgow will inevitably wander in and out of these pages like a willing change bowler reintroduced to make a point. 'Cecil Parkin,' he said, 'could bowl every known kind of ball, except the very fast – and several that were his own invention; and, as it was so often his whim, to try to fit them all into one over... His career was short, too short.'

Parkin's fame and match-winning skills in league cricket caused him to be very much in demand after the war. Rochdale, who played in the Central Lancashire League, happened to have an extraordinarily enterprising and resourceful president. They brushed aside any opposition and persuaded Cec to sign for them. It didn't need too much persuasion: they were prepared to pay him more than any league pro had previously dared to ask for. Apart from the weekly salary, he was promised a £100 benefit – exceptional for those days – and a backhander of £20 for signing.

The president was a former bricklayer called Jimmy White, an entrepreneur with a minimal knowledge of cricket but with limitless authority on affairs closer to racing stables in the north, the best restaurants and the prettiest actresses in the West End. He controlled Daly's Theatre, famous in its time; his associates included the disgraced MP and colourful John Bull maverick Horatio Bottomley, and the peerless Steve Donoghue. Jimmy White was equally liberal with gratuities and racing tips.

His flamboyant style at the initial interview utterly charmed and influenced Parkin. The cricketer was to stay with Rochdale for three years. They released him for county matches and, when he travelled to Australia for the Tests, he shared with Barnes the distinction of going there straight from the league.

There isn't much doubt about his outstanding match, of the few he played for Lancashire in 1919. In the June he was released by Rochdale for the Whitsun game with Yorkshire at Old Trafford. All fixtures were limited to two days that season; Lancashire – or rather, Parkin – won the match with seven minutes left. He took fourteen wickets. 'It was probably the greatest moment in my career,' he said so often afterwards.

Here are the figures, for once more eloquent than any prose:

1st innings: 32.3-8-88-6, 2nd innings: 28.4-13-52-8.

And that against Yorkshire, from whom he had already parted company because he lived a yard or two on the wrong side of the county boundary.

A. A. Thomson rhapsodized in *The Wars of the Roses* like this: 'Parkin, who had whipped Yorkshire in the first innings with his six wickets, chastised them in the second with scorpions. He was, as so often later, completely bewildering with his variations of pace,

104

forcing batsmen to play too soon or too late at deliveries which looked to be exactly the same speed, but were not. Though he performed many astonishing bowling feats, he always regarded this as the one which gave him most delight. Yorkshire's only consolation was a masterly half-century from Sutcliffe.'

Ah well, Herbert was always a dab hand at working out the different deliveries, as Jack Hobbs used to say.

Cecil enjoyed every minute of that match. There were plenty of affable exchanges between the opposing players out on the pitch. Parkin did his share of the talking – and chortling. A succession of Yorkshiremen surveyed their crumbling castles or gasped helplessly as they spooned pat-ball catches to the close leg-side fielders.

'Hey, Ciss, what you been doin' to theet ball, lad?'

'Don't blame ball, son. Ee, it was you, not ball!' He'd laugh, as another Yorkshireman, eyes like saucers, beat his contemplative retreat.

But Rochdale really had first call on him. He took twenty-eight wickets for the county that season at 14.89 and sent down just over 160 overs. Twice in the July he played for the Players against the Gents, at the Oval and Lord's. It was his first taste of representative cricket. 'And first time I'd been to London.'

After he had retired, he used to speak at cricket dinners and meetings. He would tell them of that maiden visit to London. 'Outside Euston station I saw this newspaper placard saying PARKIN ARRIVES IN TOWN. I just didn't know how they'd found out.' It was one of his constant jokes.

At Lord's, like any loyal North Countryman, he sniffed at the structural grandeur and hunted out those with a similar accent to say: 'No better than Old Trafford, is it?'

He made an unexceptional impact at the Oval and took nine wickets at Lord's. Someone opined that Barnes was now forty-four and must be on the way out. Parkin seemed like the best substitute – a slightly patronizing ring to the phraseology, the Rochdale pro reckoned –

and the same writer continued: 'Clever bowler that he is, no one would at present venture to place him on anything like Barnes's level.'

Again in 1920 league cricket came first. Rochdale were delighted with their signing. Jimmy White was lavish with his hospitality; Cecil eyed the beauties, like Evelyn Laye, who sat in the deckchairs on the boundary to watch special matches that the influential president organized, and kept taking wickets. His batting was by now almost an afterthought, although he could score useful runs – and quickly if needed.

Parkin was a magnet. The crowds began to note and enjoy his antics, as well as his cheeky array of bowling styles. People came specifically to watch him – and he responded to that. Loyally backed by Rochdale, he survived suspension by the League, the result of his petulant action over umpiring decisions and already discussed in the book.

The committee counted the takings on a Saturday and told him he could stay at Rochdale just as long as he wished. Their average gate used to be about £30. During one match in his first season for the club, it was up to £340. He was good for the Central Lancashire League as a whole; opposing sides benefitted financially when playing at home if they could rely on Parkin's presence. 'You don't want to play too often for Lancashire. We'll look after you,' said the ebullient Mr White.

Rochdale coveted their star and at the same time were unselfish in their dealings with the county. Parkin made five appearances for Lancashire in 190 and took thirty-nine wickets. That rate of success and another auspicious bowling conquest for the Players were enough to bring him Test recognition.

Wisden reminds us of what happened at the Oval: 'The match had a sensational opening. The Gents, batting first on a good wicket, were so demoralised by Parkin's variety of pace that they were all out for 184. Encouraged by early success, Parkin bowled in a form he had never approached in his other matches in London. He tried all his experiments and they all answered. He bowled Mr A. W. Carr with the very slow ball of which he is so fond, and beat Mr Fender who was batting away in fine style with a yorker of lightning pace. It was a great performance to take nine wickets, six of them bowled down.'

We can only speculate on what the hapless Percy made of that. It was hardly the most chivalrous of deliveries to offer to one of the game's most illustrious amateurs. But the league cricketer's liberties did him no harm at all. He was chosen to go with the MCC under Mr J. W. H. T. Douglas to Australia that winter.

The tour was a disaster from a playing point of view. Australia won all five Tests. Back home the pundits groaned, overlooking the fact that Warwick Armstrong had a marvellously balanced team at his disposal. There was the ritualistic criticism of the captain. Opinions about Johnny Douglas have always tended to be sharply divided.

Parkin was never less than outspoken about individuals, amateurs and pros. He was weak on compromise all his life. So what did he make of Douglas? 'I could never wish to travel with a finer gentleman than our skipper. I am sure my opinion is shared by every member of the England team on that tour. He was a charming fellow and words fail me in expressing my appreciation of him. Though we were outclassed in the Tests he was always cheery, just as Jack Hobbs was always a wonderful batsman on that tour.'

The chemistry clearly worked. Douglas knew the way to handle this 'old hand' from the league. He knew how to flatter him, to praise him and talk with him at the end of the day. Parkin's evaluation of his MCC captain appears uncharacteristically sycophantic. But subservience was never a quality of Parkin's. He genuinely liked Johnny Douglas, even though the Essex man had nothing to show for the tour.

In no sense did Cecil recapture the stunning successes of home. His sixteen Test wickets cost him nearly 42 runs each. That famed slow ball of his was treated with disdain, if not savagery, by the Australians. He gave the impression of lacking the confidence to vary his deliveries as impudently as back at the Oval. He'd study the mighty names in the Aussie party: Armstrong, Macartney, Collins, Bardsley, Andrews, Taylor, Mailey, Pellew, Macdonald, Gregory, Kelleway, Carter, Oldfield. . . 'every one a master', he used to say. Who could blame him for being a little overawed for one of the few times in his cricketing life.

Later he was to claim that he met 'with remarkable success' on the tour as a whole. He wasn't a failure and came next to Fender in the bowling averages. But his self-assessment is surely a trifle biased.

There was a great deal he enjoyed immensely about the tour. He'd never been to sea before and once he had conquered his sickness he enjoyed the convivial side of the journey. He took a liking to the Australians, as cricketers and people; he attended the numerous receptions and decided that many of his hosts were in the Jimmy White class, a considerable compliment. He got on well with the other players, keeping them amused with anecdotes about some of the characters in league cricket.

His best Test was at Adelaide where he took 5-60. Jack Hobbs scored a superb century in the same match. During the lunch interval, a messenger came to the dressing room and said that the State Governor would like to see the great batsman. It looked rather like an order. Jack returned, beaming, to say that he'd been presented with a diamond scarfpin.

'So that's it,' said Parkin in mock anger. 'The batsman always gets the reward. What about the poor bowler, then?'

The supposed plea from an off-spinner's heart apparently reached the State Governor. Once more the messenger arrived at the dressing room. In formal tones he said: 'The presence of Mr Parkin is required by the State Governor.'

108

Cec was out of the door before the sentence had been completed. He could do with one of those handsome scarfpins. It was all very official; a military band struck up a few stirring bars from an overture. The crowd, nearly 30,000, surged forward. And the Pride of Rochdale was formally introduced to the governor and his wife, and other affluently attired members of the official party.

Parkin was never averse to making a little speech. In his mind he was already rehearsing a few suitable remarks to acknowledge the diamond pin. The State Governor spoke: 'Well done, Parkin.' That was it. No presentation.

He made a sheepish return to the dressing room. Patsy Hendren was first to speak. 'Well, Ciss, what you got?'

'Nowt,' was the glum reply. 'I'm tellin' you – I got nowt.'

There was some suppressed laughter. Jack Hobbs came up to Parkin. 'Bad luck, Ciss. But you did choose to be a bowler and not a batsman!'

One of the spectators at Adelaide was more generous. An elderly woman gave him a basket of fruit 'for all, young man, that you've done'. The apples were pilfered by his team mates and it was probably one of those Pippins that Patsy returned from the boundary, instead of the ball, later in the day.

On to 1921 and again a few county matches. He still managed to take forty-five wickets from just eight innings. Long gone, of course, were the early days when he pushed the ball through as fast as he could and tried no fancy tricks. Since the war, at least in the matches for Lancashire, he remained at lively medium-pace but the spinning fingers, dutifully trained in the art of tweaking skulduggery in those long, painful cricketing liaisons with his selfless wife, determined the extent and the variety of the guile. Cecil Parkin was not now the Tunstall heaver, aiming for middle stump and a bit too much raw, uncomplicated zing for sluggish reflexes. He was an off-spinner. Or should we say that was a reasonable approximation of the chest of tricks he dispensed.

The Australians were here again. And Parkin, by far the best of his kind in the country, was selected for all but the Trent Bridge Test. There were sixteen wickets for him at 26.25. In front of his friends at Manchester, he took 5-38. He wasn't a pessimist by nature and didn't ponder on the fact that he'd failed to be on the winning side for any of his nine Tests against the Aussies.

Unlike Barnes, Parkin felt it was time to break with the league. He accepted that the standard would then be higher. He was already an England player and he fancied himself on that Old Trafford strip. The egotist in him asked: 'How many wickets could you get in a season for the county, Ciss?' He left Rochdale with polite good-byes and no acrimony. And he took 172 wickets in 1922 (av. 16.5), having been the first to pass 100 that first full season. Not all the pros, were ensnared by his slower ball. At times they punished him in a way no one would have dared back in Staffordshire or the Central Lancashire.

He arrived at the Waggon Works at Gloucester, where Lancashire won by an innings in two days. Gloucestershire were all out for 99 in the first innings. Parkin was bewilderingly good, finishing with 8-47 in eighteen overs. Now here was a track, he told the assembled company, he'd have happily played on every day.

'I don't know what all the bloody trouble was about. I could stay there,' came a voice. It was Gloucestershire's top scorer. Charlie Parker, from deep in the order, made 23. His remarks about his colleagues were loud and pointed. Afterwards, the gruff and basically kindly enigma slapped Cecil across the back. 'But it was also some damn good bowling from you, old son.'

From all matches in 1923 he took 209 wickets, 176 of them for Lancashire. Maurice Tate was the only other bowler to pass 200. Tate beat him to the landmark by two hours.

There was the game at Blackpool. The resort had not staged a county fixture since 1910 and was anxious to be reinstated. In fact, Glamorgan were caught on a drying wicket and were bowled out twice in a day. Parkin in the best traditions of the professional cricketer could be ruthlessly triumphant. He was unsparing in his venom. 'He had all the batsmen at his mercy,' said *Wisden,* as if trying to disguise a twinge of sympathy for the hapless Welsh county.

'Well, then, Ciss, what you think of Blackpool?'

His eyes would twinkle. 'Ee, nice place, Blackpool. Nice place fer a day out. And nice place when it's bin rainin'.'

He took 15-95 in that shortened fixture. The Manchester cricket writers had their fun at the expense of Glamorgan, and went over the top in their adulation when it came to Parkin.

Poor, poor Glamorgan. They came to Liverpool the following summer and Parkin took ten more wickets. At one point he was unplayable and captured five wickets without giving away a run. His figures in that innings: 8-5-6-6.

Right at the start of that season, when we can only charitably imply that the Derbyshire batsmen were still short of practice, he summarily dismissed eight of them for 20 runs. There was no more successful bowler in the country as he tore through the opposition in May and early June. Against the visiting South Africans he and Dick Tyldesley took twenty wickets between them.

Cecil Parkin had to be an automatic choice for the Edgbaston Test coming up in mid-June. He was – and it was his last Test. It is remembered as the Test match when South Africa were bowled out for 30 in just seventy-five minutes and seventy-five balls.

Even more sensationally than that, it was the Test match in which Parkin destroyed his brilliant career. Whether he was under-bowled and slighted, and whether he intended the public to believe he was bitterly upset at the attitude of his England captain, Arthur Gilligan, we shall shortly discuss at some length. It ranks with the domestic game's greatest controversies. Old

111

men at Old Trafford – and not only there – still stroke
their wrinkled faces and ponder the follies and the
misunderstandings of the incident.

His haul of wickets that perplexing season was 200,
four fewer than Charlie Parker and five fewer than Tate.
Leg-breaker Dick Tyldesley, a bowler with so much
heart, took 184. So he and Parkin, spinning the ball
mostly in opposite directions, were responsible for 384
wickets between them for Lancashire.

It should have been a season for celebration. Cecil
Parkin, at his own sprightly pace, was a wizard of off-
spin. It wasn't only Cardus that he sent into flights of
imagery. He was an idol among the supporters at Old
Trafford. Around the country, his presence, like that of
the endearing Hendren, induced that unspoken plea:
'Make us laugh, Ciss.' But the more discerning noticed
that after June there was less laughter in the eyes. He
was less loquacious; he showed a reluctance to juggle
with the ball. Other players, who doted on his humour
and readily acted as his feed in the banter of the dressing
room or pub, met with a declining verbal jauntiness.
He was deeply hurt – and it showed.

Parkin had every reason to expect more, perhaps
many more, appearances for his country. Lancashire had
every reason to expect many more wickets from him.
But his county career fizzled out in bitter anti-climax.

He stayed for two more summers but the sunshine
had gone from his stride. His benefit came in 1925 and
it wasn't the success one might have imagined for such
an extrovert player to whom the cricket public had
always warmed. He still made £1,880 but failed badly
in his special benefit match. Middlesex were the visitors
to Manchester and the sun considerately shone. Parkin,
ill at ease, could find virtually no turn at all. He laboured
for three wickets in the whole match and was out for a
duck. At least the spectators who had loyally come to
subsidize their favourite off-spinner were treated to an
engaging century from Patsy Hendren. Middlesex won

by 215 runs and Parkin bravely affected a smile as Patsy and his pals wished him well.

His 1925 tally for Lancashire was 121, noticeably down on the previous year. Cecil's bowling throughout his career, in league and county, thrived on garrulous good nature and a bouncy eye-winking approach to life, which showed in the way he ran up to bowl, chided a batsman on an imprudent chop or ambled up to share a drink after the day's sweat had been towelled away. When grievances engulfed him he bowled with mechanical sluggishness. The vivacity and the joy had been drained from him.

The 1926 season was his last. He was no more an integral part of the team. Lancashire won the championship and the amateurs fizzed jubilantly as they passed the champagne along to the pros. Parkin, one of the county's greatest bowlers, had already packed his bags. He was a profoundly disillusioned forty-year-old. He didn't play again after the fourteenth fixture. He had taken thirty-nine wickets from just under 260 overs. And it was goodbye. He went home and cried.

His mind was never wholly on the cricket. His memories of that final season are hazy and unreliable. He always cited Gloucestershire as his last opponent. It would have been an ironic twist in terms at least of this book. He was bowled by Charlie Parker: one more link between this pair of like minds and attitudes.

But after Gloucestershire, he played against the Australians and Leicestershire. On 25 June, he left the Ashby-de-la-Zouch ground and knew in his heart it was all over. His last victim – one of only two in the whole match – was G. B. F. Rudd. Jack Iddon held on to a difficult catch. Cecil waved an acknowledgment.

It was his 901st wicket for the county; of his nine seasons with Lancashire, he was able to play regularly only in 1922, 1923, 1924 and 1925. He came late to county and country – and he left early.

Lancashire played some marvellous cricket in the twenties and at times seemd virtually invincible as they monopolized the championship in 1926, 1927 and 1928. Strange and sad that Parkin was no more than a bit player by 1926, backing away to a deserted stagedoor and empty street. He bought an evening paper and, in the privacy of his home, read about those who had succeeded him.

Brief but bountiful had been his stay. He was surrounded by great cricketers. 'I felt proud to be in the same side as Johnny Tyldesley, Reggie Spooner, Harry Makepeace and all the rest,' he used to say. By the time Parkin was freed by league cricket to appear regularly for Lancashire, Johnny was approaching fifty. The little professional was still able to use his feet superbly; the cover drive and the late cut – he played it as well as anyone in the world – were still there to be cherished.

Cecil may have had an occasionally prickly regard for the game's more inaccessible amateurs. But his intrepid tongue was not often directed at those in his own county – nor at the inhabitants of the Old Trafford head-quarters. He'd describe the club as being rather like 'a happy family', with the minimum of hierarchical strictures. Certainly it was a good deal less snobbish than many other counties. The pros weren't cowed by the committee. Not that Parkin would have been readily cowed by anybody; and you could say the same about a few more of his outspoken team mates.

The Lancashire dressing room was a happy place, especially in the fleeting summers when he played practical jokes with the pinned-up batting order and entertained nervous batsmen with his latest version of the three-card trick. All the players had nicknames. Cecil had the uncomplimentary label of 'Pikehand'. Harry Makepeace was 'Old Shake' and Ernest Tyldesley was 'Jud'. Frank Watson was known as 'The Doc', Charlie Hallows was 'Flight' and Lol Cook was both 'Sampson' and 'Workhorse'. A few of the names were self-evident. Cook, for instance, renowned for the width and willingness of his heart, appeared always to be the bowler battling against the wind. No one heard him complain. Every county could no doubt nominate its 'Workhorse'.

E. A. McDonald arrived in 1924 from the Nelson club. Here was the definitive Australian speed merchant in many ways. He was dour and, when he wanted to be, combative. He had a beautiful action and was so light on his feet, as he sprinted up to the wicket, that the groundsman seldom found any stud marks. His new-ball coupling with Gregory, in the 1921 series against the MCC, demonstrated fast bowling at its best and most poetically rhythmic. It wasn't too much fun for the opposition.

Ted McDonald then chose to make his home in England; here, too, he was to die needlessly at the side of the road after stopping in an act of kindness to help someone in trouble. Before he gave up playing for Lancashire in 1931, just short of forty, he'd taken more than 1,000 wickets for the county. He was the attraction, the match-winner, just as Parkin had once been. They were together, in effect, for only one season.

Could Cecil have been a little jealous of Mac's popularity? Son Reg dismisses such a notion. 'Not in any sense. They were great friends. When some time later I had a benefit match in the city of Durham, he played and made sure I'd score 50. Everyone was thrilled that he turned up. He took five wickets and, bless his heart, didn't try to get me out. I must say I was a bit apprehensive about asking him to play. But Dad assured me that Mac wouldn't let me down. "Just get him a bottle of whisky," my father had said.'

It wasn't any particular secret that McDonald, like many of his contemporaries, enjoyed a drink. In the Australian tradition, carried on in flamboyant style by Keith Miller, Mac also had a marked tendency to study the form of the horses. When it came to cards, his poker face gave nothing away. He had none of Parkin's extrovert zest but would hold a bar-room of tired, relaxed fellow players enthralled by his double-jointed feats. He could bend his left arm right round his neck to touch his left ear. He could effortlessly scratch his elbow with the fingers of his same arm. And yet what he could do best of all was exhibit fast bowling as an art form. There was never a more dainty aggressor.

I suspect he was rather like Ray Lindwall and regret that I missed him. At the same time I remember the graphic summing-up of him by Cardus. Of all the miles of marvellous newsprint lavished on the game's practitioners by Sir Neville he can rarely have conveyed a more telling and perceptive flavour of a great and arguably flawed cricketer:

At Trent Bridge I saw him at the end of a sweltering day. Notts had scored nearly 400 and it was six o'clock. McDonald's captain – he was playing for Lancashire now – asked him for one final onslaught before close of play. McDonald had bowled for hours, but he bowled again. He sent down an over of brutal bumpers. An honest yeoman named Flint hit three of those bumpers for four; the last ball of the over he hooked to the square-leg ropes for six. McDonald, even before Flint's mighty stroke was finished, turned on his heel indifferently and slouched to his position in the field at mid-off. He did not even look where Flint's hit had gone. And somehow it was Flint that seemed the futile man. An onlooker in the crowd said: 'There's the Australian for you, all over.' McDonald spat on the grass – the 'Digger' from head to foot. . .

That, to me, is great descriptive writing. The narrative is simple. The insights are boundless. It doesn't matter if Cardus only pretended he heard a spectator say that.

This was the bowler who, with Richard Tyldesley, under the captaincy of Leonard Green, became Lancashire's major wicket-taker and consumer of the headline space, once the exclusive right of Parkin.

There's nothing more melancholy than a comic who laughs no longer. It is the moment for us to retrace our steps to 1924 – and try to discover why things went so horribly wrong.

116

4

Printed Words That Ended a Career

It was the anniversary of Cecil Parkin's wedding. He arrived at the Test match ground at Edgbaston on 13 June 1924 beaming with good humour and with the glint in the eye which suggested he fancied his prospects on a wicket which had absorbed a great deal of recent rain. Ernie Tyldesley, his Lancashire team mate, was 12th man. With a sentimental touch that put Cecil in an even better mood, Tyldesley went in search of Mrs Parkin and presented her with a box of chocolates.

The Test was Herbert Sutcliffe's first – and also the debut of Maurice Tate, Kilner, Percy Chapman and G. E. C. Wood, the wicket-keeper. Herbert scored 64 and Jack Hobbs 76: the overture to one of cricket's most treasured and long-running double acts. Along came Hendren, Woolley and Kilner, and England reached 438. The South Africans were hardly renowned for their attack; they'd had to enlist a chap called G. N. Parker who was temporarily playing in the Bradford League. It wasn't quite the romantic Test summons that Parker had dreamed of. . . He rushed to the ground and bowled, it must have seemed to him, right through the England innings. It was a tour-de-force performance. He took six wickets and at one stage staggered exhausted from the field. Back in the dressing room he was given smelling salts, a cold compress to place across the caked sweat

on his brow, and urgent words about his need to return
to the fray. . .

But we mustn't waste time on minor diversions. South
Africa were all out in their first innings for 30 in an hour
and a quarter. The England captain, Arthur Gilligan,
and his Sussex team mate Maurice Tate completed the
rout in a fraction over twelve overs. Here it is: Gilligan
6.3-4-7-6, Tate 6-1-12-4.

It was an inept batting display, however penetrative
the bowling. The Tourists, though demoralized, did
immeasurably better in the second innings. Catterall
reached a diligent century and the team totalled 390.
Gilligan and Tate this time took nine of the wickets
between them.

Parkin, it should be said, was having a tremendous
season. He was spinning the ball, flighting the ball and,
as we'd say today, quite often seaming it as well. He
was top of the national averages and could do no wrong.
The public loved him. Whenever he appeared to deceive
a batsman by that guileful change of pace – two or three
times an over – the murmur of excitement could be
heard all round the ground. Sometimes the spectators
would unleash their delight in peals of laughter. 'Old
Ciss' would hear them and secretly bask in what he
knew was the theatricality of his performance.

He'd assumed, from the strength of logic and not
arrogance, that Gilligan would quickly introduce him to
the attack. There is nothing more frustrating in cricket
than the experience of the bowler who never meets his
captain's eye. Frankly in seventy-five minutes of alleged
batsmanship, mistakenly billed as part of a Test match
spectacle, only two bowlers were needed. Parkin's spinning fingers were twitchy but, ah well, there was the
second innings.

'The second innings came along and I was not asked
to bowl until about the fifth change,' he later wrote. He
exaggerated the supposed slight. But Kilner, Fender and
Woolley were asked before him, after the captain and
Tate had come off. Parkin bowled sixteen overs; they

118

were unimpressive, costing 38 runs, and he failed to take a wicket. In his memoir which he published twelve years later, he wrote: 'The wicket was a hard one whereas I would rather have had one on the soft side. Mr Gilligan was probably right in not putting me on earlier. When I went on, I didn't do much with the ball.' An interesting retrospective conclusion.

He admits, however, that he noticed people laughing at him – some of them in the pavilion – when he was being repeatedly ignored by Gilligan. 'I wasn't in the least upset by that.' Not a reaction, surely, that would have been shared by many bowlers, certainly not ones at the top of the averages and known to have a mind and a rasping tongue of their own.

The 12th man, Tyldesley, and Parkin booked a taxi to take them to the station after the match; they had to travel to Gloucester for a county fixture the next day. As they climbed into the cab, Arthur Gilligan and Archie MacLaren rushed out. 'Sorry you haven't bowled much today, Ciss, but I hope you'll get some sticky wickets soon,' said the captain. They shook hands. Neither realized they would soon be locked in an unedifying conflict.

At Gloucester, a few of the Lancashire team were in playful, if not exactly diplomatic, mood. 'See you got played in the Test match for your singing, lad!' Parkin insisted that the leg-pulling and the semblances of sarcasm didn't bother him.

Now we come to the incident which in effect destroyed his affection for the game and put his career into inexorable reverse. On the last day of the Gloucestershire match, a Friday, he received a wire from the *Empire News*, the paper for whom he wrote a weekly column. They were getting anxious because he had not yet sent them anything. They needed it that day.

This is Parkin's version of what happened: 'At the tea interval I went to the press tent and asked if one of my Lancashire journalist friends who travelled round with the county team would oblige me by putting a few lines together and wiring them. I did this because I was pushed for time. As a rule I wrote the articles myself and posted them to London. On this occasion I didn't indicate what subject I wanted to be written about. I left the matter to my press friend to compose. Next day we were due to play Leicestershire and we had to travel up from Gloucester late at night. My pressman had gone on an earlier train and when I saw him next day I didn't ask him what he'd written about.'

We will discuss the ethics and the dangers of ghost-writing in a moment. By coincidence I had somewhat similar requests made to me in that exposed and billowing press tent at Gloucester, years later. The mechanics of the trade are well known to me.

Cecil lay in bed at Ashby-de-la-Zouche, reading the Sunday papers. He turned to the sports pages of the *Empire News*. The match report recorded with enthusiasm that he had taken his 100th wicket of the season the previous day. But almost immediately he was distracted by the black banner headline that dominated the page.

CECIL PARKIN REFUSES TO PLAY FOR ENGLAND AGAIN.

It was so unreal in its ostentatious flourish that he couldn't at first take it in. For the rest of his life he repeated: 'Was this supposed to be about me? I hadn't said anything of the sort. And I hadn't authorized anyone else to say it on my behalf.'

This is part of what was said in that *Empire News* article, under Parkin's name:

On the last morning of the Test match there were 105 minutes' play. With Catterall hitting so finely it was necessary for the England captain to make many bowling changes. During those changes I was standing all the time at mid-off, wondering what on earth I had done to be overlooked. I can say that I never felt so humiliated in the whole course of my cricket career. Nothing like it has ever happened to me in first class cricket.

I admit that on Monday I was not at my best, but why should Mr Gilligan have assumed that I would be worse than useless on Tuesday? It has been said that the wicket was too hard for me. In that case, why was I ever played at all? A first-class bowler with any sort of reputation has that reputation to keep, like anybody else.

I can take the rough with the smooth but I am not going to stand being treated as I was on Tuesday. I feel that I shouldn't be fair to myself if I accepted an invitation to play in any further Test match. Not that I expect to receive one.

Could anything have been more final or self-destructive? All over the country, the *Empire News* was proclaiming Parkin's disenchantment with Test cricket – and his England captain. It was sensational stuff, presented in a way to produce the greatest journalistic impact. And even as the Lancashire bowler was sitting in bed gazing with, as he maintained, disbelieving eyes at his so-called indictment of Gilligan and saying that he had had enough of Test matches, the phones were buzzing with belligerence at establishment level. The game's hierarchy didn't tend to favour this brash, laconic style for their Sunday morning reading. But the word had already spread around the old-boy network. 'Have you seen what this Parkin is saying. He's having a go at Arthur!'

It was, of course, a preposterous thing for a professional to do. He couldn't win. He was taking on the amateurs – but appeared willing to destroy himself in the process. The force of his emotional argument was also lessened because it seemed to be founded on one personal slight. It was the voice of a man whose pride had been hurt.

Or was it? Parkin tells us that when his anger that Sunday morning had momentarily subsided, he dressed and rushed to the hotel where the Lancashire journalists were staying. He confronted his 'ghost' and asked why he had written such an uncompromising attack on the captain and implied that Cec would never play for England again. He claimed that the response was: 'It's the best thing that's ever happened, Ciss.'

Parkin, flustered and in despair, couldn't seek out his county captain Jack Sharp for guidance. Sharp, with another ironic twist, had gone to Lord's that day as one of the England selectors, to choose the next Test XI. The selectors were angry and Sharp was embarrassed; when it came to the team, they showed their newly found contempt for Parkin by not even mentioning him. Back at the ground next day, he called the dejected bowler to one side. 'You've made an awful bloody mess of this. Why do you let someone else do your writing for you?'

A retraction clearly had to be put out. Jack Sharp helped Parkin draft a statement for the Press Association, who promptly relayed it to every corner of the country. The statement said that the last thing Parkin wanted to do was criticize a captain for whom he had a great admiration. It looked like a clumsy and desperate cover-up. The damage had been irreparably done.

Lancashire's next match was back at Manchester, against Sussex. Arthur Gilligan didn't play. His absence was probably diplomatic.

The county committee summoned Parkin for an explanation. He was sheepish and ill at ease, so different from cricket's jaunty comedian and 'bag of tricks'. That article, he repeated, was written without his consent. The views that were published weren't his.

It turned into a cross-examination. 'Well, Parkin, you say you didn't write the piece, so who did?'

'I – I can't say.'

'Why not?'

'Because it would get him into trouble. If I ask someone to do something for me, I must stand by what he writes and accept the responsibility.'

The name of the journalist who ghosted that exceedingly contentious column for Cecil Parkin was never revealed, though some of his colleagues knew who it was. In his memoir, Parkin wrote: 'I determined to keep my mouth closed whatever the results to myself. But I never spoke to that pressman again.'

Maybe we should pause and consider the implications. Johnny Clegg worked for the *Manchester Evening News,* covering the matches of Lancashire home and away. He was a respected cricket writer, popular in the press box. His match reports, which appeared under his initials, were for the most part balanced and reasonable. He was a sound journalist and though he relished the occasional 'human' story that was strictly a matter of runs and wickets, his style was straight rather than racy.

Clegg was something of a legend among Manchester journalists. He was a short man with a distinctive moustache, and there were many good-natured anecdotes told about it. Friends claimed he liked a drink. One night, after leaving the Press Club in Manchester, he was riding on the tram along Piccadilly when his benevolent and slightly blurred gaze was directed to the side of the road. 'Elephants!' he exploded. 'There are elephants loose in Manchester. . .' Johnny blinked a few times and then went into a silence, attributing his hallucination to the last glass of ale. But there were elephants on the street. The circus was in town. 'Cleggy' and his elephants remained for years a favourite story in the Press Club. The ageless Dick Williamson, himself already a legendary figure among the sports journalists of Bradford, only vaguely remembers Clegg; but he recalls that particular Tale of Piccadilly, passed on through a couple of generations of pressmen, with absolute clarity.

I have talked to old, canny North Country journalists, and young ones. Almost without exception they found it hard to believe that an experienced cricket writer like Clegg, who was so close to the players and was trusted by them – despite the occasional unpopular story he had to write about them – would have been naïve enough to ghost the Cecil Parkin article without, in that specific case, discussing the content with the player.

Sportsmen and their 'ghosts' build up an intimate

relationship. Usually a few stray thoughts from the player are enough to provide the writer with the basis of a first-person story. The 'ghost' has come to know the way his sportsman thinks, the phrases he uses, the hobby-horses he rides. The public, some of whom are excessively gullible, are quite happy to go along with the arrangement, it appears. It's good for circulation and supplements the player's wages. Professional bodies and trade unions within the newspaper business are often less happy. That is another story altogether.

Johnny Clegg didn't write the Parkin column on a regular basis. Cec Parkin's son, who reasonably believes his father was wronged and pilloried over the incident, says: 'You must remember that players had continually to rush from one game to the next. Transport was often a problem in those days. There were occasions when people like Dad had to rely on journalists to help them out. I feel he was badly let down in this case.'

It isn't contested that Cec Parkin went across to the press tent to ask Clegg to help him out. They had some discussion and it seems likely that they had a cursory word about the column's content. Parkin's recent Test appearance and enforced indolence were the obvious topics. Cecil was known to be smarting from the taunts and teasing. Clegg, as a loyal Lancashire reporter, felt the Pride of Old Trafford was appallingly under-bowled.

The copy had to be written that same evening and wired to London. So there was a time problem and Parkin was already on his way to Leicestershire. But would the experienced and reputable man from the *Manchester Evening News* have dared to put such scathing words into the mouth of his subject without some kind of nod of acquiescence from the cricketer who was being paid to come up with strong, outspoken views each Sunday?

I know, from close-hand knowledge, something of the mentality and journalistic philosophy of Fleet Street's sporting 'chancers'. They dispense fiction as part of the highly competitive game played out on their respective sports pages. Their staccato prose is beaten out at the behest of distant desk-men who visualize the headlines first. But not one of cricket's more insensitive scribes would have killed off Parkin's Test career in the way it was done – without his authority.

We shall never know whether it was all a matter of misunderstanding and naïvete. We do know that it filled the enigmatic Parkin with remorse and bitterness.

He was asked by his county to send a personal letter to Arthur Gilligan. A few days later there was a reply:

My Dear Ciss – Thank you very much for your letter and apology re the Birmingham match. I really feel sorry that you, by writing in the papers, have handicapped yourself so severely. We have always had very pleasant relations on the cricket field, and I shall never let anything interfere with good sportsmanship and fellow-ship. I feel sure that, if you had really given it thought, you would have taken time to consider the consequences of criticising my captaincy at Birmingham.

No doubt you felt entitled to your opinion, but I wish you had spoken to me personally about the matter instead of slanging me in the press. I could, anyway, have told you whether I agreed with you or not.

I feel awfully sorry that you have got into trouble with the authorities over this affair. Anyway, Ciss, I much appreciate your letter and accept your apologies. The whole matter, as far as I am personally concerned, is now closed. I shall never refer to it again.

Best of luck to you and to Lancashire.
Yours sincerely,
Arthur E. R. Gilligan.

It was a generous letter, while making it clear at the same time that Gilligan felt hurt. Later in the season, Lancashire played Sussex again. People held their breaths: both Gilligan and Parkin were playing. The private correspondence between the two had been no business of the public. Then when Lancashire took the field, Arthur Gilligan walked alongside Parkin with arms around the shoulder. It was the public gesture of reconciliation. Spectators noticed it and applauded.

But the controversy lived on – for years. In his auto-biography, E. J. (Tiger) Smith wrote of Parkin: 'He was a temperamental character and he didn't take kindly to not getting a bowl for long periods. It was a silly thing writing that article about Gilligan because Parkin wasn't fit to bowl. He had an injury to his arm and back, and the Aston Villa trainer was summoned to massage him. Parkin's outburst in the Press was unprofessional and he didn't deserve to play for England again. He'd forgotten that the captain must ultimately be the sole judge of things on the field.'

That was a new aspect. But Parkin never mentioned any injury that handicapped him at Edgbaston. He wanted to play – and he certainly wanted to bowl. The presence of the Villa trainer was not a consideration.

The Times, seldom a thunderer by inclination on the sports pages, couldn't keep out of this spot of trouble. It took them six days to offer an opinion. Then the cricket correspondent demurred affectedly and slipped in this delicate reprimand. 'Into the personal reasons that may have led to the omission of Parkin from the XI (for the next Test) I have no desire to write much. It is a great pity that he rushed into print. He would have done far better to keep his grievance, legitimate or otherwise, to himself.'

Cardus was to write: 'The course of genius never did run smooth. Parkin – a genius of cricket if ever there was one – always possessed the defects of his qualities . . . But none of us, surely, is going to harp on these defects.'

And, in another place, Cardus returned to the Birmingham Test: 'Cecil, wrongly advised, protested that he had been harshly treated. "I didn't mind", he said, "Mr Gilligan and Maurice Tate going on straightway after getting South Africa out for 30. But in the second innings, I was never looked at for hours . . . and the score mounting up every over . . . and Mr

Gilligan bowlin' with his knees in the blockhole!" ' The master writer, who savoured a choice phrase, went on to rhapsodize over Parkin's vivid description of the England captain.

In redressing the balance, the observations of Rex Pogson, in his essay on Lancashire, are timely. 'To the popular Press, Parkin's outspoken and sometimes outrageous comments on his contemporaries, particularly Test captains and MCC administrators, were a source of revenue. Like many people gifted with the ability to wisecrack disconcertingly, he was not always wise in his choice of time and subject, but his repentance was usually sincere and disarming. Diehards who had cherished the belief that cricket professionals like Victorian children should be seen and not heard, found him irritating. But his hold on the public's loyalty never wavered.'

That is quite true. Cec Parkin was subjected to some very cruel forms of abuse following his remarks about Gilligan. Telegrams and letters were sent to Old Trafford; some were jokey and even satirical, others were infinitely more pungent. Many were anonymous. The backlash left him dispirited and, he claimed in his blacker moments, vilified. He utterly lost his enjoyment for the game. The county club saw how morose he had become and tried to lift his morale.

'You've got a lot more wickets to take for us yet,' they told him, and they knew he wasn't listening.

Suddenly he said: 'I've had enough. I love Lancashire but there are too many people around who don't want me. For the rest of my life I'm going to be blamed for something I didn't say.'

He had planned to play county cricket for six more years. Now he was gone, back into the league. He joined Blackpool in 1927, took over a hotel and played cricket as an amateur. Blackpool won the Ribblesdale League and he took 138 wickets, more than anyone previously in the League. No one mentioned Gilligan. He stayed for three years; then he had two as the pro with East

Lancashire CC at Blackburn, before moving to Tonge in the Bolton League. Gout put an end to his cricket in 1935 when he was the Levenshulme professional.

Cec Parkin ran a succession of pubs and hotels in Lancashire. He put on weight, would talk cricket till closing time and watched the county on occasions. His affection for the Old Trafford set-up never really lessened. He'd go back to help with the coaching. He travelled miles around the county, under a popular *Daily Dispatch* scheme, giving coaching lessons to scores of aspiring young county players. Invitations to the humblest village club, as a speaker, were hardly ever ignored. As if purging the distasteful rumpus from 1924, he put a great deal back into the local game. He was making a point to those who whispered behind his back that he was too avaricious.

In his last season, for Tonge, he was nearly seventeen stone. By then he bowled leg-break and googlie. The arm wasn't as high but the joyful cunning was just as unbridled. Son Reg would occasionally play against his father. 'Go and get some exercise, Dad,' I used to say. Father would give him a long, significant look. 'I've had enough exercise to last me, playing cricket over the years. Now I'm taking it easy.'

It pleased Cecil to see his son follow him into county cricket with Lancashire. He was a capable all-rounder 'but there were too many good players about at the time'. He left Lancashire in 1934 and finished up in the league, playing mostly in the Central Lancashire League. 'I once got 60 against Gloucestershire and was told that if I'd reached 100 that day I'd have been awarded my cap. But we had a big staff. With a cap, you went on top money. Counties didn't give caps too freely!'

In one match for Lancashire, Reg Parkin bowled a full toss and was hit for six. George Duckworth went up to him and said: 'You're trying to do like your dad. But he bowled 'em on purpose!'

Reg Parkin chuckled at the memory. 'Dad once

128

chucked up a full toss to Percy Fender and it was put down deep square leg's throat. He'd bowl long hops if necessary ... anything to get a wicket, if the ground was big enough.'

Cecil was fifty-seven when he died in Manchester Hospital. He had cancer of the throat. It was a big funeral at Manchester Crematorium. Wilfred Rhodes, George Hirst, and Harry Makepeace were there: and many other old cricketers, and members of the Lancashire club. The ashes were scattered over the wicket at Old Trafford. It was not something Reg approved of. 'To me it smacked too much of commercialism. Grief should be more private than that.' Cardus wrote that Cecil's wife laid a red rose on each end of the wicket.

Part Three
MacBryan, John
Crawford William
(1892–1983)

Born Box, Wiltshire, son of a doctor who specialized in mental health. Educated Exeter, where captain of cricket and Cambridge, where he won his Blue in 1920. Played for Somerset 1911–31, frequently heading the batting averages. Scored 18 centuries and renowned for attractive and correct style. Also represented Somerset at rugby, golf and hockey, and played for England in the 1920 Olympic Games – at hockey. Played once only for his country at cricket (and because of bad weather did not bat).

'He's a right fine bat and looks to me more like a Yorkshire pro than a Somerset amateur'

Wilfred Rhodes

1

Never Wanted to be a
Cricketer at All

Unlucky Jack. . .

That was what he called himself and the impression,
based on compounded strands of misfortune and quirks
of fate, some of them self-induced and not all entirely
standing the retrospective test of logic, grew into an
inexorable obsession.

He was one of the most correct and attractive batsmen
of his day. Few played the late cut better. He was a
master technician and regularly headed the Somerset
averages. Yet he played only once for England and,
because of the bad weather, didn't face a ball. He
suspected that a few jealous fellow amateurs blocked his
way with varying degrees of subtlety and disaffection.

His Cambridge Blue was given him almost grudgingly
after he had been overlooked completely the previous
summer. The Varsity match, when it was his turn,
should have been a spellbinding contest between some
of the finest players ever brought together for the event.
Rain and restricted hours ruined the atmosphere and
the cricket.

At school he had a superb cover drive. Then he put
his shoulder out when playing fly-half for Bath. He was
never able to hit the ball properly off the front foot
through the off side again.

He would have liked to play for Middlesex and told
Frank Mann of his aspirations many times. 'Just can't

133

be done, old fellow. Qualifications all wrong.' So Jack, born in Wiltshire, was saddled with Somerset just because his father had some property in Bath. His enjoyment with Somerset was minimal. 'Too many bad players,' he'd say repeatedly. And then with a viperine strike of the tongue: 'Too many bad amateurs.'

Outside his cricket, there were many other reasons – more absorbing ones – for him to feel unlucky.

His father, he vehemently believed, had little love for him and chose to obstruct his professional career. Jack wanted to be a doctor who specialized in neurology and mental disorders. His father, who ran a mental asylum, actively discouraged him. The uneasy relationship of the pair embittered the son and Jack became more and more convinced in the late years of his life that his father's frigid and unhelpful attitude to him sprang from intense jealousy. After Jack had been taken prisoner in the First World War there was the chance of an exchange repatriation, involving him and a German doctor. Old Man MacBryan, according to the son, did nothing about it.

Jack was especially close to his mother and she died when he was young. His favourite brother, Tod, died in the war. Friends used to joke that he'd have really liked to go to Eton or one of the top public schools. He went to Exeter because his father was told 'there isn't any buggery there'. He married a Gaiety Girl and it was a disaster. She soon fancied someone else. And eventually, through no fault of his own, he lost all his money on the Stock Exchange. But he shouldn't have been a stockbroker at all: and he knew it.

Do we go on? Surely not; the list is a formidable one and the point has been made.

During my visits to him in Cambridge and in his many letters to me, he returned unfailingly to the theme of parental attitudes. His mother died of a fever when he was ten. She was a gentle and loving soul. 'Being her first-born, I suppose she made a great fuss of me. That brought upon my head the extreme jealousy of my father.'

134

Doctor MacBryan was a successful and rather a vain man. He was bald and insisted on wearing a hat most of the day, indoors as well. He ran the asylum, at Kingsdown House, Box, with professional skill and probably a modest sense of business. The private patients, whose wayward mental conditions varied enormously, came in the main from well-heeled families. He came from Ulster stock and had an Irishman's relish for conversation. Some of his jokes were in somewhat dubious taste. He enjoyed the social side of cricket and was sparing in his compliments about Jack's ability. The father never missed the Weston-super-Mare festival.

Robertson-Glasgow remembers him vividly in his autobiographical *46 Not Out*. 'A short walk away from the ground were the golf links. There, peace was to be found in the evening, balm for any failure on the cricket field; and in the lounge, Doctor MacBryan, Jack's father, would be sitting, benevolent and conversational, in a drain-pipe collar that kept stiff up to his ears.'

Young Jack took an acute, curious interest in what went on at the asylum. He eavesdropped on the case histories and watched, from a distance, the pathetic confusion and bizarre behaviour of the patients. He dipped into his father's books. This, he decided, was a challenging career worth pursuing.

When I was sixteen, Sir Robert Armstrong-Jones had come to dinner. He said to my father: 'Mac, you have a chap here (me) made for our branch of medicine.' Sir Robert, accompanied by another Harley Street neurologist Dr David Ferrier had come down to see a patient at a fee of 106 guineas each (London to Bath 106 miles). The young woman, I remember, had seized a child from its pram on Bournemouth pier and thrown it into the sea from where it was rescued. She found her way to father's loony bin.

Despite that encouraging opinion of my promise from Sir Robert, father had me removed from a school class working for the 'Little Go' – entrance to university – and directed me towards an army career.

I joined the 13th, The Prince Albert's Somerset Light Infantry, but on reaching my twenty-first birthday I resigned my commission and made my father send me to Bart's to study medicine. I passed the first M.B. a month before the 1914-18 war, when I rejoined my regiment for the Special Reserve.

In my situation I was entitled to opt out of the Services. But I was too funky to do so, and my father did nothing about it. A couple of years later, after I had been taken prisoner, I became quite friendly with the German camp officer. When he heard I was a medical student, he advised me strongly to write home to obtain influence for an exchange. I did but my father again did nothing.

At the time the Rt Hon. Walter Long, of the old-established Wiltshire family, was President of the Board of Trade. From his days in the Harrow team he was very keen on cricket. Later I often sat with him at Lord's watching some match or other. Without a single doubt his influence could have been brought to bear on the question of a war-time exchange.

I quote at length from Jack MacBryan's letter to me partly because it offers a fascinating insight into the network mentality: but more so because it reflects a son's contempt for his father.

We now arrive at JCW's business affairs. They were not for a moment spectacularly successful. He was a socialite in that he went to parties and liked the good things of life. Against that he had few personal possessions – and not much spare cash.

It was too late, after the war, to retrieve the inclinations and boyish enthusiasm for his medical studies. After Cambridge he worked for a time as the personal assistant for the chairman of a leading hotel group. He had plans to learn the business from the bottom up but such vague intentions were never substantiated. His bank balance usually had an ominous look. Ultimately

136

he joined a firm of stockbrokers but compulsory retirement came at sixty-five and he was far from a rich man.

MacBryan later became one of three partners in another venture. It failed miserably. 'I've heard from any number of people on the Stock Exchange and they all agree it wasn't Jack's fault,' a loyal friend told me. That was probably true. The other partners died. 'Poor old Jack was left on his own. He was hammered when he was eighty. He lost virtually every penny.'

He cancelled his copy of the *Financial Times* and become increasingly insular. He retreated more to his upstair room in the extensive, well-furnished terrace house in Cambridge of Mrs Cecil Mackay, which he shared. Cussed as ever, he bought the *Daily Mirror* and occasionally checked on the cricket in Cecil's copy of *The Times*. He completed the *Mirror* crossword, did his embroidery, continued to plan the flower border in the back garden and wrote copious letters. His correspondence with Sir Len Hutton gave him pleasure. He wrote to good friends in the Somerset Wyverns like Royse Riddell, who grew up watching his cricket at Weston's Clarence Park, John Durman and Edward Francis. The only Somerset player he wrote to was Bill Andrews, 'the best cricket coach I've ever known'. It no doubt appealed to Jack that Bill had been sacked four times by Somerset: someone with that track record clearly had many human virtues. The pair had found themselves together at Blackpool during the last war. JCW was in charge of cricket for the Royal Air Force there – and Bill was in the side. In the letters they exchanged years after, the extrovert all rounder would recall the days when he operated the Weston scoreboard and Jack late-cut four exquisite boundaries in an over from Maurice Tate. Another Andrews memory was of the two of them, the Squadron Leader and the gangling corporal, squatting on the pavement in Blackpool, eating fish and chips. I'm not sure that the erstwhile sophisticate and bon viveur would have willingly confirmed the veracity of that romantic and unlikely after-match banquet. But it was a favourite tale of Bill's and brought mutual chuckles as the two cricketers, both renowned for their splendid handwriting, despatched their reminiscences between Weston and Cambridge.

'JCW was a lovely bat, one of the best Somerset ever had. But he was so BLOODY unlucky,' Bill would tell me a score of times. Here was a witness I'd listen to any time.

I can delay the cricket no longer. Sammy Woods often assured Jack he was the best bat in the country. It was just the trifle of an exaggeration, influenced by geographical allegiance and maybe a dram or two of whisky. Dar Lyon was almost as unequivocal in his praise. John Daniell was less effusive; and so was Peter Johnson, a fellow stockbroker whose handsome batsmanship was equalled by his immaculate and often riveting appearance before the match started. He was known to turn up in top hat and morning coat, much to the irritation of JCW.

In another chapter I shall discuss MacBryan's lack of love for Somerset and most of the county's amateurs. Peter Randall Johnson was his particular *bête noire*. He saw him as the man who influenced the Test selectors to look elsewhere. 'Johnson told them I was too damned bad tempered.' The pair seldom exchanged more than perfunctory and coolly polite conversation in the amateurs' dressing room.

When Middlesex came to play Somerset at Clarence Park one year, Johnson was acutely embarrassed to discover contraceptives in all his pockets. He considered that to be a practical joke of bad taste. The joker was MacBryan; and I have the story on the discreetly amused authority of Gubby Allen. JCW knew Johnson for the kind of 'upright' chap he was. The incident, which brought collective guffaws, carried a cruel streak.

This is primarily a chapter about MacBryan's lack of luck. Johnny Douglas, a good personal friend with whom he stayed and shared decanters of port into the early hours during visits to Essex, thought his guest deserved better from fate – and the selectors. The sentiments were shared by Leveson Gower . . . and many of the Somerset professionals.

'Daniell and the rest didn't know what to make of my kind of batting. It was different from what they'd been used to. It wasn't in the airy-fairy public school and university tradition. It was based on footwork, science and application.' He would tell me this, pause and add: 'That's why I was so proud to be likened to a Yorkshire professional.'

It happened at Scarborough in the early twenties when MCC were playing the champion county. Yorkshire were mean as ever, bowling away as if their life depended on it. There was no concession to Festival cricket. But at lunch, the slight, dapper MacBryan was still resolutely there. He had made no semblance of a mistake. The feet were right, the timing was perfect. And there were no capitulating flourishes of the bat as if this were an end-of-term romp squeezed in on the way to the station and the 'vacs'.

He knew he'd done well. The North Country wiseacres would be approving. Then, as he touched his light blue Cambridge cap to acknowledge the warm applause of the crowd, he heard Wilfred Rhodes say to the umpire, George Hirst: 'Aye, that one looks more like a Yorkshire professional than a Somerset amateur.'

No compliment in JCW's cricketing career pleased him more. He repeated it many times to me, not to brag but to emphasize his own philosophy to batting as encapsulated in Wilfred's one pithy sentence.

Jack liked playing against Yorkshire best of all. Once at Hull ('It was during a dockers' strike, I remember' – his memory was as ever almost faultless), the Somerset innings had virtually collapsed in an undignified heap. Robinson, Macaulay, Waddington, Rhodes and Roy Kilner were all, in rotation, in marvellous form. Any batting side had valid reasons to make excuses. MacBryan almost carried his bat that day. As he walked in, the Yorkshire players lined up to applaud him. They accepted that he never once looked like giving his wicket away. In class and technique he was a world apart from the rest of the Somerset team.

But before dwelliing on his cricket over 156 matches and sixteen centuries for the county he disliked so much, let us take a glimpse at the matches when he won his Blue and his Test place. True to form, the gods ganged up against him.

The 1920 Varsity match should have been a gem. Cambridge had two future England captains, Percy Chapman and Arthur Gilligan, and at least three more – Clem Gibson, Hubert Ashton and George Wood – who were sounded out about going to Australia on the next tour. Douglas Jardine went in No 1 for Oxford.

Jack MacBryan, back from the war, had been 12th man in 1919 and now he was in. Some said he should have been in the year before. His record was a good one. Then he went down and immediately cracked a big score for Somerset against Gloucestershire. Within twenty-four hours a telegram arrived for him, signed by three prominent members of the Cambridge side. 'They made it clear they thought I should have played against Oxford.' Ah, well. . .

There was this business of J. S. F. Morrison, the Cambridge skipper, and his ostentatious habit of drinking sherry out of a beer mug. 'I saw it during a match at Fenners and I said very loudly I didn't think much of a chap who did that. Morrison was a prewar Blue but I thought his behaviour was disgraceful and I said so. My remarks reached his mother, a charming woman who lived in Cambidge. She asked me along for tea. I can tell you she approved of what I'd done. But, yes, it may have cost me my place in the Varsity match.'

He was selected in 1920. The two sides were laden with talent. Oxford also included F. W. Gilligan, G. T. S. Stevens and R. C. (not yet 'Crusoe') Robertson-Glasgow. It was too much to hope that Jack would be lucky. There was no play on the first two days and only two hours on the third. 'I think it was George Wood who persuaded them to keep going on the fourth day. Bloody fool!' The match eventually gave way to the Eton and Harrow fixture. The most pointless Varsity contest of all ended in an indeterminate draw.

Oxford made 193 and Cambridge's reply was 161-9. 'Father' Marriott took seven wickets for Cambridge. But it was a game without a heart. MacBryan was out for five, officially stumped by Gilligan off Bettington. His version, told with a wry, weary smile, offers a mild relief of humour. 'I wasn't only stumped. I was bowled and caught as well. I got a touch to a very good ball from Reg Bettington as I played forward. It hit the wicket and went on into the wicket-keeper's hands. Then, with my foot still raised, the Oxford skipper also took the remaining ball off!'

Several years ago I discussed that frustrating match with JCW for an article in *The Cricketer*. He was already a frail, old man, sitting in his bedroom-window chair. He was in his dressing gown, chain smoking as usual and pretending to be blasé as he talked about former cricketing days. In truth he was loving it. The venom was still there. The eyes were twinkling. We shared a few bottles of his favourite beer and I promised to bring a bottle of claret next time. 'You will come again, won't you?' he said, almost poignantly. Bill Edrich had called quite recently.

MacBryan directed me to a corner of the room where from a haphazard and dusty pile of memorabilia I found a faded group photograph of the 1920 Cambridge team. Famous names, all. He held the rectangle of frayed cardboard in his hand. 'Tell me about them,' I said. His mind, clear and perceptive as ever, sped back sixty years. This is what he told me, without hesitation or revised opinion:

Mm...Yes...'Father' Marriott. As good a leg-break bowler as I've ever seen. Absolute class, and the WORST fielder. They used to have to hide him in the field. Don't know why they called him Father. He was an oldish-looking chap. Played for Kent, of course.

Chapman and Gilligan. Let's take them together. Well, all I can tell you is that there was an old don at my college, Jesus, who never missed a match at Fenners. Of that fine Cambridge side, he said, the two members who lacked leadership qualities were Chapman and Gilligan!

N. E. Partridge . . . He was a wonderful all-rounder. A medium-paced swing bowler, probably faster than medium. Yes, a magnificent cricketer. Played for Warwickshire.

Clem Gibson was an opening bowler who was asked to go to Australia. Bowled outswingers, not exaggerated ones. But batsmen were also apt to be surprised to find their leg stumps on the ground. No one quite knew why.

Now that's Gilbert Ashton, the finest cover point I think I've ever known. And he had only one thumb. Lost the other in the war. It didn't seem to make any difference.

George Wood, our captain, was an utterly brilliant wicket-keeper. Used to stand up. Completely fearless and incredibly good. He went in first but was really a goodish No 8. What chance did I have?

That leaves Hubert Ashton and myself. Hubert was a splendid amateur bat but he went out to India and that ruled out Australia. Me? You know about me, old chap. Unlucky Jack. Here, let's have another bottle of beer.

Con Johnstone went in first with Wood and No 1 for Kent. Quite top-class. But I honestly don't think Geoffrey Brooke-Taylor should have been in. Came from Cheltenham, you know, the same school as Wood. That may have helped. He was still a pretty good player.

I come now to Test recognition, so brief and unnoticeable that it was gone for good in the flickering of an eyelid. JCW had topped the Somerset averages in the early twenties and looked like doing so, provided he was

142

sufficiently available, for the next decade. No one questioned his distinctive skills. In 1924 he was chosen to play against South Africa at Old Trafford. He discovered he was down to bat at No 3, after Sutcliffe and Sandham, but before Woolley and Hendren. At Manchester, alas, the skies were laden and the rains came. Just two and threequarter hours' play was possible. Jack took his place in the slips and hardly touched the ball. He was one of the very few Test batsmen never to walk to the wicket for his country. Unlucky Jack was never selected again.

He was one of *Wisden*'s Cricketers of the Year in 1925. That token appearance at Old Trafford earned not a sheepish mention. But the tributes were generous and the article ended: 'He was at the top of his form all last season and was a strong candidate for a place in the MCC team for Australia. Not being chosen for the trip, he went out to South Africa with Mr Joel's XI.'

MacBryan's private information was that he had been chosen for Australia. 'The chairman of the selectors told me Peter Johnson said I didn't have the right temperament. What he should have said was that I was utterly disgruntled with the Somerset set-up.'

Yes, of course, he had every reason to harbour a few grievances as he sat and pondered in that window seat of his bedroom in a Cambridge side street. He was absolutely right about the pathetic collective skills around him at times in the Somerset team. He was absolutely right that some of the amateurs didn't like him very much. But there were flaws in his personality and these encouraged antagonisms.

Geoffrey Cuthbertson, who briefly captained Northamptonshire, was a constant and loyal friend of JCW. Although younger, he had first met Jack at Cambridge. 'He was wearing his Sandhurst blazer on that first meeting, I remember. I looked up to him. He was intelligent, amusing and didn't suffer fools. Jack was perhaps an awkward fellow but we got along right away. Unlucky Jack, did he say? Bless my soul! Just look at the sort of successes he had in various sports – and the wonderful life he was able to lead, despite the disappointments.'

Mrs Cecil Mackay was equally loyal. 'One of Jack's old schoolmasters told him that his life had been a tragedy – and Jack, of course, agreed with him. But that was sheer rubbish. He was so good at games. He played rugby for Bath, Richmond and Somerset. He played golf at county level. He was good enough to play hockey for his country in the Olympic Games. He was a super cricketer. What a marvellous start that gave him in life. And there was so much more for him to enjoy. 'Good heavens above, he wasn't unlucky. . .'

2

Coaching in the School Dining Room

Jack MacBryan was never in too much doubt about the worst innings he ever played. He was fifteen and made 'tons of runs' for Wiltshire Boys against Somerset Boys. The heavily whiskered committee members of Somerset were well represented at Taunton that day. Their intended interest was a tall, powerful fast bowler called Humphrey Critchley-Salmonson, born in Dorset and educated at Winchester. Public school sports masters and coaches, especially those with Winchester ties, were claiming rather grandly that he was an emerging demon bowler. The Somerset county elders were there to confirm the exciting rustle of the grapevine. Poor Critchley-Salmonson tried harder and bowled faster. His towering schoolboy build and windmill ferocity made no impression at all on a slender, phlegmatic young batsman whose feet were almost instinctively in the right place and who nullified any merits the bowler may have had.

It was always intended that Critchley-Salmonson would end up with Somerset. He was nearly as fast as anything Somerset had at that time. In fact, he went off to the Argentine and came back an infinitely less hostile bower. He played only fourteen matches for the county and took twenty-four wickets.

In contrast, few had heard of this lad MacBryan. He captained his school, Exeter, at cricket and his father was known as 'that doctor from the mental place', apt to pop his head round the pavilion door when there were matches at Bath.

But he was the boy who dominated the match between Wiltshire and Somerset. 'Doc' MacBryan basked in the complimentary remarks and let it be known, with the right touch of discretion, that he was the father. By now he was sitting next to Somerset's principal administrator and president H. Murray-Anderdon.

'You say you live in Wiltshire, Doctor. Such a pity about that.'

'Well yes, only just over the boundary.'

Murray-Anderdon, a practised hand at bending rules, looked the doctor up and down. 'I don't suppose you have any property in Bath, now?'

'But, yes.'

And so J. C. W. MacBryan became a Somerset player. It had never once occurred to him that he would. From the outset, it held little appeal. Even at prep school, he used to say: 'I'm going to play for Middlesex or Surrey.'

He refused to give up the idea of switching counties. He pestered Frank Mann about it. 'I'm not sticking my neck out,' said the Middlesex captain. Significantly, when MacBryan left county cricket he severed all apparent links with Somerset. The county, for their part, lost his address and he was conspicuously absent from the centenary celebrations in 1975.

I have mentioned the prep school. It was St Christopher's, in Bath, where the headmaster, Mr Charles W. Trask, had his own effective and unorthodox method of coaching potential cricketers. Little Jack was much impressed.

'I suppose I was seven or eight when Mr Trask would line half a dozen of us up in a large dining room. We all had a bat in our hand and were told to adopt the proper stance. From the other end of the room he'd go through the motions of bowling overarm – without a ball. When the imaginary ball had just left his hand, he'd shout 'Play!' We were expected to play a normal forward stroke with the left foot pointing at the pitch of the so-called ball. Then we had to hold the position while he came forward to examine us, one by one.'

The headmaster was a pedant and a purist – and a very fine coach. Jack MacBryan attributed much of his neat, correct style to the instruction he received in a school dining hall.

He made his debut for Somerset during the closing days of August in 1911, when on leave from Sandhurst. The fixture was at Bath and 'Doc' MacBryan, who must surely have had more paternal pride than the son acknowledges, took the pony and trap from the asylum to watch. The trainee soldier scored 19 in both innings against Lancashire. Harry Dean twice bowled him off his pads. Jack made only a handful of appearances up to the outbreak of war. His batting, suffering from lack of match practice, was undistinguished though he did once hit 61 in 1914.

In 1919 he scored 95 in one match for Somerset as a rude rebuke to Morrison who had picked the Cambridge side and left him out. In 1920 he made his first century for Somerset. It was at Bournemouth after the Varsity game. I turn again, almost at random, to Robertson-Glasgow, whose felicitous prose astutely tells so much of the man without ever once losing the priceless thread of humour.

And so to the return match with Hampshire at Bournemouth. I spent the evening before it exploring with Jack MacBryan. I wonder how many of those who chance to see his name in cricket scores remember what a great player he was?

That evening, Jack was in one of those moods of *en-tout-cas* preparedness in which a man tends to laugh at the morrow and criticise other people's hats. Soon after leaving the hotel, we were nearly run over by a car which, Jack remarked, was proabably in the pay of the Hampshire committee. At the next corner the same thing happened. Jack shouted one of those terms calculated to cause all but the more experienced London taxi drivers to draw up within a few lengths. There followed an altercation with the charioteer, whose fondness for alcohol was now manifest. Jack drew off his coat, but there the matter rested. As the driver receded, taking what revenge he could out of his gears, Jack turned to me and said: 'Good. Now I'll make a hundred.' And he did.

I imagine the incident embarrassed Crusoe, a gentle poet who argued only about the nature of things when he penned a philosophical aside. JCW, nearly thirty now and hardened by the war, had sharpened his waspish tongue and was ready to trade insults with drunken drivers in a public place.

There was another century against Hampshire the following year, this time at Weston-super-Mare, where, as now, the tropical conifers enclose the ground. Hampshire bowled Somerset out in an hour and a half for 61 on the first day – and won by eight wickets on the second. JCW tugged at his Cambridge cap and visibly despaired at some of the gauche, synthetic batting going on around him. He was the county's top scorer with 16 in the first innings; he then battled quite superbly to score 101 out of 179 in an unavailing attempt to make a game of it.

Some of the overweight amateurs blustered their way out of the ground, blaming the wicket. Weston hadn't been given a county match until 1914 after all; and then came the war. The wicket is still being blamed. It has been libelled, slandered and blasphemed, accused in turn of being a fickle and vicious Jezebel and a slumbering, lifeless old dog.

Robertson-Glasgow liked it, for all that. 'Of all county grounds, Clarence Park is about the smallest and most intimate. It was the home pitch of Jim Bridges, the Somerset bowler, and there in club matches he liked to come out strong as a batsman. "If only they knew that you and I, Glasgie, are as good batsmen as any in

Jack MacBryan and Harry Makepeace, going out to bat for The Rest against
England at Lord's in 1923

JCW's father, watching cricket at Bath with Sammy Woods

Sammy Woods, Jack's great hero

Early schooldays (1905) at St Christopher's Bath. Centre back row is headmaster Mr Charles Trask, a big influence on Jack's cricket, and next to him is Jack's brother, Tod. JCW is second right in the middle row

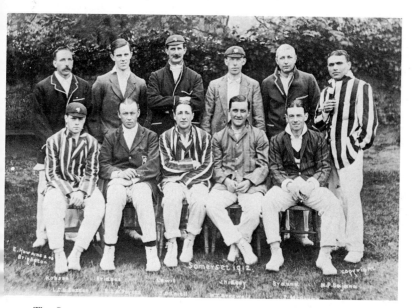

The Somerset team of 1912. Back row: E. Robson, J. Bridges, A. Lewis,
H. Chidgey, L. Braund, M. Bajana. Front row: L. Sutton, E. Poyntz, J. Daniell,
W. Greswell, J. MacBryan

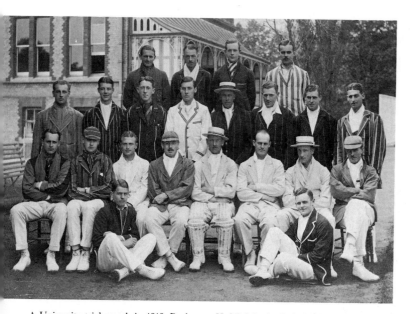

A University trial match in 1919. Back row: H. M. Morris, J. C. W. MacBryan,
G. B. Cuthbertson, H. G. Doggart. Middle row: T. A. L. Brocklebank,
G. O. Shelmerdine, H. W. Taylor, J. P. Bennett, A. E. R. Gilligan, M. D. Lyon,
C. P. Brooke-Taylor, C. R. Browne. Sitting: C. P. Johnstone, G. A. Rotherham,
G. Wilson, J. S. F. Morrison, G. E. C. Wood, G. A. Fairbairn, Hon. F. S. Gough-
Calthorpe, J. H. Naumann. On ground: G. D. Huband, G. Ashton

J. C. White, a Somerset colleague (left)

Not long before his death, JCW presented an embroidery of his old school's (Exeter) crest to the headmaster, Mr Geoffrey Goodall, who visited him in Cambridge. It marked the school's 350th anniversary. The School bursar, Col. Peter Weeks, is on the left

Gents XI which played (despite the fog!) at Scarborough in 1924

the Somerset side, except possibly Dar Lyon and Jack MacBryan". . .'

He should have known that R-G always fancied his batting and did open the innings for his county.

I know so well from personal experience what Crusoe meant when he said something odd was always happening at Weston-super-Mare. I could write a racy, oddball sporting memoir all about the place. Journalistically it's the most fruitful of territories.

Wasn't it at Weston that Percy Fender registered a complaint on behalf of the Surrey amateurs that there wasn't enough room in the hotel bedrooms to swing a cat? The hotel manager's reply was: 'I didn't realize Surrey had come to the resort merely for cat-swinging.' It wasn't the pre-war Grand Atlantic, surely.

Over the next three years JCW showed up the paucity of batting in the team. He topped the averages and scored nine more centuries. Some within the club thought he was getting a little above himself. He claimed John Daniell was too old to be captain and had his favourites. 'He's a good manager, excellent at booking hotels, things like that.' JCW was a good deal less generous about Daniell's tactical and playing ability, forgetting the notable innings and the brave fielding at silly point off Jack White's bowling.

By 1923 he was scoring 1831 runs. He opened with Harry Makepeace in the Test trial at Lord's and compiled an orderly, almost flawless 80. In the September he went in first with Herbert Sutcliffe at Hastings, Uncapped v. Capped, and his 53 was top score. There was also a half-century for the Gents against the Players at Scarborough.

We should pass quickly over the winter 1924-25 tour of South Africa. Charlie Parker was also in the party; he'd already made his protest over protocol to the ship bursar, you may remember. There were five unofficial Tests. JCW played in all but one and scored a mere 44 runs. He scored centuries against Natal and Border, and relished the receptions.

With not too much money either in his bank account or his back pocket, JCW needed in 1925 to devote some time to work away from the cricket field. He played in only eight county matches. They included the famous and much documented match against Surrey at Taunton, where Jack Hobbs first equalled and then surpassed W. G. Grace's record of 126 first-class centuries. By now we know by heart every uncharacteristic, stifled drive, every detail of the agonizing catch off a no-ball; the weeks of personal torment that preceded the feat . . . and Fender's flourished brimful of non-alcoholic fizzy that followed it.

Submerged in the ecstasy of the occasion is another innings that deserves attention. MacBryan hit a beautiful 109 in Somerset's second innings. He dominated an opening stand of 184 with Tom Young, that frail, talented, much underrated all-rounder whose lungs finally gave up on him and led to a premature death soon after he gave up playing.

The Times, whose cricket correspondent had thundered down for the historic event of Hobbs's achievement, didn't ignore MacBryan. 'He played a magnificent innings. One of the best of his career, without a flaw. . .'

Jack Hobbs led the applause when JCW was out. The Somerset amateur, whose unqualified regard for The Master was that of every other player in the current game, just once accompanied Hobbs to the wicket. They were playing for the Rest of England against Yorkshire, as the champion county. 'I was immensely proud.'

I had known for a long time how much MacBryan would have liked to play for Middlesex. But not till one of his last letters did I realize how near he came to joining Surrey. Anything but Somerset, it seems.

'By the summer of 1914, remember, I had resigned my commission in the 13th Somerset Light Infantry and gone to St Bart's Hospital as a medical student. I wasn't at that time a member of Lord's so I joined Surrey at the Oval and took nets each evening. Who should be the bowlers one day but Hayward and Hobbs. They must have quite liked the look of me. Next day I received a letter from the former Surrey captain, Lord Dalmeny as he was then. He wanted to know if I was qualified for Surrey. I immediately began to make enquiries about lodgings in the county. Alas, in a few weeks' time war broke out.'

There were three more centuries for him in 1926, his last full season. The one that pleased him most was against Yorkshire at Taunton. Neither John Daniell nor Jack White was fit. MacBryan led Somerset, putting on 184 with his only close friend in the side, Dar Lyon, for the second wicket. They both reached their hundreds, both passed 1,000 runs for the season. It was the highest stand against Yorkshire that summer.

It was a match of immense enjoyment for JCW. He was pitting his wits against the great Yorkshire bowlers – as skipper. And he was doing it with Lyon, out there in the middle. 'Dar was a magnificent player but we weren't very often in together. Then he was apt to give me one of those meaningful looks and tell me to stay down my end. That meant he wanted me to play the slow bowlers!'

From 1927 onwards there wasn't much cricket to speak of. MacBryan tried to get on with his work. His disappearance, gradual to start with, from the county scene was a matter of regret. There were rumours that he'd had too many rows and that his face didn't fit any longer. 'I'd simply had enough of the people I was playing with. They'd never learned from their mistakes – they still played like schoolboys. They were, or at least some of them, were dull and unsophisticated. I'd been a prisoner-of-war and had gone through some varied and absorbing experiences but not once did anyone at the club ask me about them. Maybe there was a bit of guilt in one or two cases. J. C. White was excused going into the services because he was a farmer and couldn't be spared. But as soon as the war was over, it seemed, he was off to Australia.' Such things rankled interminably;

151

others must determine whether Jack MacBryan was a petty man.

He did engender affection in spite of his toxic tongue and unfeeling barbs. When he met Sammy Woods in a London club off St James's Square and told him that he'd decided to give up county cricket, the big, tough, jolly Australian broke down and wept.

MacBryan's last first-class game was for the MCC against Gentlemen of Ireland in 1936. He opened the innings, pretended he could middle the ball and made 6 and 1. There are better memories.

For Somerset he scored 8,372 runs at an average of 31.01. In all, his first-class aggregate was 10,322 runs and eighteen centuries. Not bad, in a limited career, for a batsman who couldn't play the cover drive. That rugby injury, suffered against Pontypridd, also ruined his throwing arm as an outfielder. He stuck to the slips and gully instead, and took 126 catches.

Jack MacBryan hated ugly shots. He batted without flamboyance or theatrical flourish and must have been good to watch. Everyone says so, including his enemies. Close friendship can blur judgments but the words of Geoffrey Cuthbertson shouldn't be rejected on that account. 'Apart from Hobbs, Jack MacBryan was the best bat I ever had the privilege of watching from the other end. He made an ordinary player look like a plough boy.'

He batted in a different way from many of his contemporaries. Every ball he received was an intellectual exercise to be conquered. The intense concentration was etched on his strong Ulster face. For six balls an over, cricket was an unrelieved battle of the mind: in the same way as it is nowadays for another Somerset man, Peter Roebuck. He'd have liked Roebuck, also a Cambridge graduate who perhaps takes the game to the almost self-defeating extreme of 'thinking about it' rather than playing it at times with a little more instinct.

JCW had a prodigious knowledge of cricket in the technical sense. He studied the individualistic strengths of all the great bowlers he knew he would have to face. He relished the challenge of countering spin by the nimble use of his feet and he deplored what he saw as the decline of the art of slow bowling in the modern game.

'In my view, the greatest asset a bowler can possess, however, is pace off the wicket – never mind what his speed is through the air,' he reiterated in a dozen letters. 'If you were playing Jack White, for instance, you might have adjusted to his pace through the air, so to speak. But often you found that the ball had struck your stumps before you'd completed your stroke.'

Farmer White was famous, of course, for that deceptive zip off the ground. So he was for his mastery of flight, though he hardly spun the ball at all. 'I put that down to the coaching he had from Ted Tyler, a similar type of bowler.'

As a purist, MacBryan was overtly angry with himself when he miscalculated the stroke he should play. He returned to the pavilion, huffing in self-rebuke. 'In the match against the Australians at Taunton, I kept hitting Richardson past mid-on for four. The off-spinner was giving me no trouble at all. Then he bowled me one that didn't turn. Result? A catch for the wicket-keeper off the right-hand edge of the bat. Jolly well bowled . . . bloody badly batted!'

He warmed to the stylists and worried aloud about the risk-takers. Lionel Palairet was his kind of batsman. Palairet had given up two years before Jack first played for Somerset but he had watched him with infinite joy in the school holidays. In the case of Harold Gimblett he had reservations. JCW would go along to Lord's, after his retirement from the game, to see what all the fuss was about. Was this engaging young agricultural upstart going to live up to all that romantic nonsense which emanated from Frome?

'A fine young player he turned out to be. His off-drive was done to perfection. But I was concerned about the way he played the hook shot. You just didn't do that at headquarters, in front of the hierarchy. I wrote to Gimblett and suggested he might be rather more cautious in his use of the hook – at least at Lord's. I got no reply.'

That disappointed him. 'I was only trying to help his career.' How was he to know that poor, old Harold already had other things on his mind?

MacBryan had an endearing inconsistency when it came to some of the players he favoured. Who'd ever call Sammy Woods the most exquisitely balanced and consummate artist of batsmanship in the business? Or even the larger-than-life Sir Timothy O'Brien?

Woods keeps coming back into this story because he was the greatest single influence on JCW. The younger man may have been both sophisticated and rather snobbish. But he doted on Sammy's raucous, boozy, happy style. Before he gave up in 1910, the convivial Australian was a habitué of the county ground and the Castle Hotel or the George – and a few other taverns in both Taunton and Bridgwater. As a reluctant form of exercise, he was known to walk from Bridgwater to St James Street on the morning of a match. He chattered away to everyone he met in the roadway. He was without side – and at times without too much money. He played skittles with the enthusiasm of a rustic. At Bridgwater Fair, he once or twice stepped into the boxing booth without an ounce of belligerence in his nature. No one will ever quite know how he made it to Cambridge but he did bowl terribly well for them. He played rugby for England, and cricket for both England and Australia, a show of conflicting loyalties that amused him and generated a score of stories. In the end he was more Somerset than Sydney. His family did come from this country in the first place.

And yes, of course, as Jack would remind you with pride, Woods was a great all-rounder. He captained Somerset for twelve years and scored eighteen centuries for the county. He bowled his heart out and deserved that drink. One county exile told me with disguised affection: 'When I was a little girl, the impression I

always had was that his breath smelt of whisky.'
MacBryan never disapproved of a glass or two, if the
heart was in the right place.

'Sam joined the Somerset Light Infantry, you know.
Served in the Camel Corps in Egypt. Was riding a camel
one day when it suddenly set off in the direction of some
intimidating cactus shrubs with wicked spikes on them.
He sensed the danger and threw himself off. Broke a leg,
too. That's why he always had a limp. . .' There was
admiration in Jack's voice. The limp got worse in
Sammy's case. He played with a good deal of pain
towards the end of his ebullient career.

On my visits to Cambridge, Jack MacBryan would
put aside his embroidery – his 'sewing' as he called it –
and talk for hours about cricket, pretending at the same
time that he didn't have much time for it anymore. His
voice stayed on one phlegmatic pitch but the eyes gave
him away. He still loved cricket more than he wanted
me to believe.

'Sam Woods . . . well, yes . . . What he didn't know
about batting, never mind bowling, isn't worth
considering. He knew absolutely everything and it was
a joy and an education to listen to him. I remember so
well a morning at Taunton where I was in all kinds of
trouble against Tate. Just couldn't work him out at all.
I was not out when we came in for lunch. And there
was Sam, sitting in his usual place by the entrance. He
gave me one of those looks. 'What the hell do you think
you're doing out there?' I'd been missed several times.
I blurted out that I just didn't know which way the ball
was going.

'He called for several old cricket balls and immediately
led me to the nets. Then he began bowling underarm at
me with great skill. He taught me to stop my stroke
directly I saw the ball was going away to the off. Then
he had a go at the leg stump with the ball that veered
inwards off the pitch. All the time he was giving me
invaluable advice . . . "Play this one at the last pole of
the net" (on side) . . . "And that's the one to go for four

to fine leg" ... I went without my lunch, eternally grateful to Sam. What an education for me!'

'I had a number of conversations with Maurice Tate. He was as honest to me as to others who discussed his great bowling art with him. Tate simply didn't know which way the ball was going.'

JCW spent hours in the company of his mentor. He retold anecdotes involving Sammy with almost biblical awe. The two of them were together in the bar with George Geary after he had taken all ten in an innings for Leicestershire at Pontypridd. George probably expected a more straightforward compliment from the big-muscled Aussie than an arching of the bushy brow and: 'Is that really the best you can do, old dear?'

'Well, yes, I suppose it is, Mr Woods,' said George, who considered his haul of sixteen wickets in that particular match with Glamorgan hadn't been bad going at all.

'Did better than you, George. Once got 200 wickets in an afternoon. My brother got another 107.'

MacBryan would retell the story with great glee. It seems that the two boys once rounded up several hundred aboriginees – and then bowled them out in a statistical orgy.

What happened in a village match one Sunday at Orchard Portman in Somerset was even more of a favourite tale.

Mac found himself going in first against Lord Portman's side. Sammy was the umpire and before there were many runs on the improvised board the Somerset batsman, renowned for his classical style and minimum of batting flaws, was being given instructions by the rather portly figure in the white coat.

'It's time you were out, Jack. Hit Eddie [Lord Portman] up a catch.'

JCW was taken aback. But this was a country house match and no reputations were at stake. He did as he was ordered. Alas, the aristocratic and none-too-athletic Eddie put the catch down.

156

Umpire Woods looked pointedly at the batsman. 'He ought to have held it. So you're out!'

The somewhat bewildered opening bat wandered back to the little village pavilion. 'How were you out?' they asked, with puzzled expressions.

MacBryan thought hard for a logical explanation. 'Because Sam said so!' The unconventional edict was accepted without question.

JCW, who lived through an era which produced some great cricketing names, nominated Tate as the finest bowler he ever faced. When it came to extolling No 1 batsmen, he went for the beknighted Timothy O'Brien and Len Hutton. 'They both had that marvellous ability to play that apparently normal stroke through the covers and, because of perfect timing, it would flash to the boundary.' His list is oddly incomplete but reveals both perceptive and eccentric viewpoints that are very much part of the fascination of the man.

He exchanged letters with Sir Leonard and the pair obviously shared many views on the technique of batsmanship, the diminishing stature of the game and coaching in schools.

Sir Timothy's remains a name that stimulates chuckles and recitations of feats that bordered on folklore. He had every reason to bask in the Oxford win over the Australians in 1884; after all, he cover-drove his way to 92. He once rattled a century in eighty minutes for Middlesex against Yorkshire at Lord's. There was his always lively batting and mobile fielding; and later the successes of his All-Ireland XI.

And, yes, he was a character. Just before the 1914 war, JCW found himself playing in a match for Lionel Robinson, the South African magnate, against Oxford University. The Robinson all-amateur team was a formidable one, including Archie MacLaren, B. J. T. Bosanquet, the capable South African pair, Schwarz and Pegler, and the Irish baronet.

Jack and Sir Timothy, fearfully out of practice, strode in to open the innings. 'I believe there's a chap playing for Oxford who swerves the ball from off to leg,' said the Somerset man by way of conversation.

'Oh, is there now! We'll see about that. . .'

Oxford had von Melle, of South Africa, playing for them. He, like Somerset's Bill Greswell and one or two others, was an exponent of the innovatory in-swing bowling.

Sir Timothy had hardly held a bat in his hand for the best part of eight or ten years, apart from a token net at Lord's. He was away most of the time on his estate in Ireland. Memories of his dashing days with Middlesex were beginning to fade.

In that match for Lionel Robinson he scored 90 in the first innings and topped it with a century in the second. His opening partner, who long preceded him back to the pavilion, was left marvelling at the recaptured timing. It was as if he'd never given up county cricket.

W. G. Grace's eulogistic assessment of Arthur Shrewsbury has been much quoted. Sammy Woods passed on to MacBryan a slightly extended version. 'When WG was asked who was the best batsman in England, he scratched his head and said that, after him, it was either Shrewsbury or Tim O'Brien.'

It does seem that O'Brien was utterly untroubled by a type of bowling he'd never come up against before – and he was fifty-three at the time.

'I must tell you,' recalled MacBryan, 'that when I called him for a run to extra cover, he'd turn it down and ask me to hit the ball harder. When he did the same in the next over, he'd scuttle down the wicket like a rabbit.'

There was a sumptuous dinner organized during the match. He came across a woman who was telling fortunes and he held out his left hand which she examined with meticulous care. She gave him an odd look and announced: 'You are going to have thirteen children, Sir Timothy.'

'And that's where you're wrong, Madam,' he retorted.

'I already HAVE thirteen children.' He turned theatrically on his heels, MacBryan chortling away at his side.

Sir Tim, with his title, his family estate and his worldly ways, was a name dusted off in Jack's days of affectionate and misty nostalgia. So was Johnny Douglas, as he called him with the chummy regard of an erstwhile intimate. 'Johnny and his great friend, 'Shrimp' Leveson Gower, were very keen to see me in the England side.'

JCW liked to move in that kind of circle and indeed he did it with a natural sophisticated panache. When a friend of Shrimp's, Sir Rowland Blades, was Lord Mayor of London, Jack was asked along to dine at the Mansion House. 'Rowly Blades had been a terribly good slow bowler . . . probably the slowest ever!'

The Somerset opener was also the only member of the county team ever to be invited to stay with Douglas when they were playing Essex at Leyton. There was always much cricket talk after dinner as they systematically emptied the port decanter. 'I remember one evening when Johnny placed his elbows on the table, rested his face in his hands and gave me one of those enigmatic smiles. We were talking about the way he chose to vary his deliveries.'

Douglas, no doubt looking for a late-night compliment, said: 'You know which way I go, don't you Jack?'

His dinner companion, in good humour, decided it was a technical point from which virtues could be equally shared. 'No, not really, Johnny. I play you off the pitch.'

There was a silence and a penetrative look from the Essex captain. Then: 'You're a bloody liar.'

They exchanged lingering grins and drained their glasses. For the last few minutes of the night before they retired to bed, the pair stuck to boxing and the Olympic Games. Douglas relived his great scrap with 'Snowy' Baker in the middleweight final. MacBryan talked of his one hockey appearance in the Games at Antwerp and the fact that Somerset small-mindedly, as he saw it, wanted him to put his cricket first.

Within the Somerset dressing room, JCW's emotional proximity to the others was a matter of intriguing contrasts. If he didn't like some of the amateurs, neither did they like him. His unpopularity, where it was evident, was in part self-induced. I gained the impression, in my meetings with him, that he sometimes wondered in retrospect whether a few of his judgments were too severe.

His relationship with John Daniell, about which I shall have more to say later, was uneasy and at times frigid. Yet, as if belatedly consumed with guilt, MacBryan also went to pains to cite the more stirring qualities of the county's former captain, secretary and president. Well, yes, he was a fine organizer . . . and, yes, he did play damn well when he scored 174 and 108 in the game with Essex in 1925 . . . of course, yes, he was a great rugby man, good enough to captain England three times, and no one could touch him as a selector. . .

In a letter to Royse Riddell, of the Somerset Wyverns, not long before Jack's death, he wrote: 'The work of John Daniell in getting Somerset going again after the First World War, with no funds available, deserves some credit.' It sounds like grudging praise; but from him, submerging his prejudices, it has the stamp of the true compliment.

The fact was that too many of the Somerset amateurs irritated him. According to him they weren't interested in culture or real conversation. Far worse, however, in his tetchy view: they couldn't play. They arrived at Taunton on a conveyor belt, wearing their impressive public school caps and larking about as if they were still in the Lower Third. As for the older, more established amateurs, he found he had precious little in common with them.

Prejudice certainly blinded him to merits. He failed to see the wristy elegance in those 10,000 or so runs and seventeen centuries by Peter Johnson for Somerset. He saw instead the silk scarves and the 'swanky manner'.

P. R. Johnson held too much sway on a nudge-nudge basis with the authorities when it came to representative honours. Here was the man who he believed, out of jealousy – he was a fellow stockbroker, significantly – stood between him and a greater recognition at the highest level.

MacBryan used to retell this story. 'I was in the hotel with Peter Johnson on the evening after I'd batted through the innings against Yorkshire at Hull. I knew it was a thoroughly good knock. Johnson was on the Lord's selection committee and he showed me his idea of the team for the Gents XI. At the top he had 'J. L. Bryan (or MacBryan)'. I turned to him and said "Damning me with faint praise, I see".'

JCW would quickly offer a conversational postscript that he didn't necessarily think he was better than Kent's Jack Bryan. But you knew he smarted at the way Johnson, for whatever psychological motive, set out his favoured selection.

When it came to J. C. White, MacBryan was more ready to extoll his virtues as a poker player. He acknowledged the considerable bowling skills but maintained that Jack White was too selfish as a player and was embarrassingly over-bowled.

'The way Somerset bowling was handled in his day, at least while I was in the side, was often deplorable. There seemed to be a 99 per cent reliance on White to the detriment of all the other bowlers. They became disgruntled and it showed. Do you know that, under Percy Chapman, he sent down forty-seven overs in a day against the Australians on tour?

'Of course he was a very great bowler. I can't help thinking that his qualities as a poker player helped him in his wiles as a slow bowler. He never managed to spin the ball but he didn't need to. Yet he seemed to go on bowling for ever, over after over. Why wasn't Tom Young, a top class and underestimated off-spinner, used more? Young had a marvellous cricketing sense both with the bat and the ball. He was scarcely ever called on to bowl, which may have suited him, I fancy, as he was inclined to a slightly lazy nature.'

There's an enthralling unpredictability about MacBryan and his personal judgments. To the surprise of many, he had a high regard for Edward Stephen Massey Poyntz, briefly his captain at Somerset before the 1914 war. Massey, as he was known, played just over 100 times for the county from 1905 onwards. He once scored 89 and took altogether eight wickets.

'No, he wasn't much of a player but I rather liked him. He did quite a passable job in the slips alongside Len Braund. And he wasn't at all a bad captain. I once stayed with him at his Clifton flat in Bristol. The most remarkable thing about the place was his Coat of Arms. "Good God, whatever's that?" I asked him as soon as I went into the flat. I'd never seen anything like it. Massey explained that his family could be traced back to William the Conqueror.'

And now we come to the Somerset professionals. Romantically he used to say he'd have liked to be one of them. He made no bones about his wayward lack of affluence. 'I jolly well wish I'd been paid for playing.' That was an attitude very much in conflict with the general philosophy of the amateurs' changing room.

There was always an ambivalence about his glimmer-ings of liberalism. The social division that had the amateurs and professionals emerging from separate directions at the start of play did at times bother him. 'Do you know my most vivid memory of my Somerset debut? Going out to bat with Len Braund at one point. He gave me a little push at the gate so that, as an amateur, I'd precede him on to the pitch. And me really just a boy. I never felt such a bloody fool in all my life!'

He mostly liked the pros: Jim Bridges, the Weston licensee and good stock bowler (who also played as an amateur); Ernie Robson, who was still bowling unchanged at the age of forty-nine and who pocketed

£50 from Dar Lyon's father after hitting a winning six against Middlesex; Ted Tyler, who'd left the county staff by the time Jack arrived but who arranged considerately for a cricket bat and full kit to be sent through the Red Cross to Mac during his PoW days; Talbot Lewis, a professional goalkeeper and the best billiards player in Taunton, and like 'Robbie' another fine Somerset all-rounder. 'Later when he used to come and watch us play, I'd go and sit with him. I don't think any of the other amateurs ever bothered.'

The professionals, for their part, would demonstrate their loyalty and regard for JCW. So, less surprisingly, would his closer friends. Geoffrey Cuthbertson recalls a match when he played alongside MacBryan for Cambridge against the Army. Percy Chapman was critical of the way the runs were coming in the second innings, including Jack's contribution. Cuthbertson noted the way Percy was shouting the odds.

The criticism, he felt, was unjustified. 'Sit down, Percy,' he exploded at last. 'If you could bat half as well as Jack MacBryan I'd like to see it.'

Just a final thought or two on this complex Somerset amateur. He was a fine player and he liked people to recognize the fact. Once, before I had met him, I gathered a few facts and impressions together and wrote a vignette on him for a book about West Country cricketers. I was generous in my praise but implied that he was 'on the fringe of the Somerset elite'. The phrase caused him to topple out of his trusted armchair with indignation. 'Good heavens, what's the fellow thinking about? On the FRINGE, did he say?' He forgave me and from that supposed slight there developed what for me was an enriching friendship.

The acerbic sting in every other observation, the utter candour and the abiding cynicism were irresistible.

In one of his last letters to me he wrote: 'I hardly like to confess it but my first-class cricketing was done for general publicity. I'd become a stockbroker as you know for private clients and I'd hoped to pick up a few of 'em in Somerset. In the event, I got two only. . .'

I simply don't believe that was the only reason he became a county cricketer. It was just another way for him somehow to justify joining Somerset.

3

Stylist – without a
Cover Drive

Jack was born in the July of 1892, the oldest of five
children, in the village of Box, a few miles away from
Bath, and just inside the Wiltshire border where his
father ran the private mental hospital for women. Only
the one sister, Mrs Ivy Hardy, survives. A brother, Tod,
was Jack's favourite but was killed in the war. Another
brother, Gerard, was by far the most flamboyant and
probably the cleverest. He was intended for the Navy,
only to fail all his exams at Dartmouth. In a later period
of his life he was personal assistant to the Rajah of
Sarawak. His was the dominant personality among the
children. The lifestyle was extravagantly colourful.

On the father's side, the family was Irish Protestant.
The grandfather, a cavalry officer, died from cholera in
India. Jack's father completed his medical qualifications
and was briefly a ship's doctor. He subsequently took
over the private asylum at Kingsdown House, Box.
There was a large staff and all the patients were private
ones. It was never a very profitable business. 'The Doc'
found plenty of free time to view the cricket.

He was described by someone who remembers him
well as 'something of a club bore'. The young Royse
Riddell was once invited with his family to Kingsdown
House for an evening meal. 'I can still see the senior
nurse poking her head round the dining-room door and

informing Mr MacBryan: "The ladies are all quiet now, sir." It was an odd sensation.'

Jack's mother died from a fever when he was ten. The family came from Reigate and the business was that of East India merchants. He missed his mother dreadfully. She had always given him, he claimed, the warmth and love that he looked for in vain from his father.

He started at Box Infants School, where he was taught good handwriting. He and his brother, Tod, were given extra lessons. They moved on to St Christopher's preparatory school, where cricket bats figured prominently on the curriculum and Jack was soon showing an aptitude for the ritualistic game. Exeter was the senior school selected for him. He was a conscientious scholar and ended up captain of cricket. In later life, when the signs of the snob surfaced, he gave the impression it wasn't the school he'd have chosen. But he had Exeter to thank for the sound all-round grounding and his bent for languages.

In March 1983 he was visited by the headmaster and bursar. They had come to Cambridge officially to thank him for the delightful embroidery he had done of the school's coat of arms. He was very moved that they should want to come and see him. 'What a lark!' he told me with boyish joy. That was the side of him we saw too seldom.

On the strength of his time at Sandhurst he was able to go to Cambridge for five terms after the 1914-18 war. He retained his links with Jesus College and a retired don used to call on him when he had gone beyond the occasional afternoon at Fenners. While at Cambridge he was something of a celebrity because of his cricket and the fact that he'd been taken prisoner in the war. He involved himself with the social aspects of College life; he was secretary of the Hawkes Ball, earning himself a reputation for fund-raising.

He returned to Kingsdown House less frequently. It was one of the oldest recorded 'asylums' of its kind in the country. The patients couldn't have asked for a more restful retreat. There were the lawns and the gardens, and the Downs nearby. But by now Jack had accepted with some bitterness that fate – and a paternal shove – had directed him away from mental health as a career.

MacBryan not only represented Somerset at cricket. He did the same at hockey ('only the once, I didn't think much of their style'), golf ('I daresay I got in because I was a decent cricketer') and rugby. His tennis wasn't bad either, though his predilection for a partner was a pretty woman with a title.

His greatest skill, apart from cricket, was on the rugby field. He was a tidy, uncomplicated fly-half with a safe pair of hands and a reliable kick for touch. There was no lack of courage in the tackle. Once when playing for Richmond against the Harlequins, Adrian Stoop joined him at tea. 'He came and sat next to me. Then he told me that if I'd had an eighth of an inch on my legs, I'd have gone far. The trouble was that I was a quick starter but had no real sustained pace.'

On the day in 1914 when his shoulder was dislocated during a fiery game against Pontypridd at Bath, a doctor was called out of the crowd. 'I was carried to the touch-line. They put me face down and the doctor knelt astride me, to heave the shoulder back in place.'

Jack played rugby again. But the cover drive had gone, more or less, for good.

He was a smallish, good-looking chap out on the cricket or rugby pitch. The reporters were inclined to call him dapper. He lacked, however, the extrovert demeanour, now apparently known as charisma, that would make him a natural hero. Yet I found one Taunton supporter, Reg Holway, who confessed that he'd always idolized JCW. 'As a boy, I used to watch him put a shilling on top of the stumps and challenge groundstaff lads to hit it. His defence was so perfect that they never did.'

If anyone should be tempted to dismiss MacBryan for the negative qualities and inherent pessimism that he was apt to show to the world, his shoulder injury compounded by the chips that he chose to carry figuratively on that region of his anatomy, it's as well to look at his wartime experiences.

As a young subaltern he was wounded and taken prisoner in the retreat from Mons. He spent three and a half years as PoW, offsetting the deprivations with a spirit of resourcefulness and resilience. He taught Russian officers arithmetic – in French. He studied butterflies in a German forest. And he had some good luck, too, ending up playing cricket in Holland.

Jack recounted his wounding near Ligny-sur-Combresis like this: 'Suddenly the enemy was becoming visible, advancing in extended order in many lines, the nearest five hundred yards away. It was then that the order to retreat was received and, whilst doing so at the double, shouting "Steady, steady" to my men, I was shot in the right buttock. It was an inglorious moment. The bullet didn't lodge but passed through the groin. Almost immediately my right leg lost all feeling and I couldn't go any farther. Somehow a few of us dragged ourselves a mile and a half back to the village where a casualty station had been set up. I was given some drugs and woke next morning to discover that my genitals had swollen to a most interesting size.'

The daughter of the local mayor, 'a lovely young woman, well-made, charming face' worked tirelessly. She'd had to cut Jack's trousers off. Now she was back with a pair of her father's civic pin-stripes. 'They went round my waist twice but in view of what I discovered I was now carrying around with me, it was just as well the new bags were on the large size.'

There was one abortive escape bid, schemed by the comely M'm'selle. MacBryan was in five different camps. When allowed out on parole at the last one to walk the forests, he started his butterfly collection and was cross with himself for failing by just three to catch all the beautiful native species. He was saddened to leave his collection behind when hustled away at the end of the war. He was less bothered about parting company with his violin. 'Several of us were given lessons by the son of a Belgium bandmaster. I was dreadful but it passed the time.'

His days as a prisoner weren't too bad. Other young officers said he made better use of his time than anyone else. He kept himself mentally sharp. He leaned on his latent powers of self-reliance. He took advantage of whatever social privilege was going – and there was a fair amount if your documents showed you had the right education and were a doctor's son. The Germans were always an impressionable race.

For his part, he acquired a genuine admiration for the Germans as organizers. He was also rather impressed with the military ritual and pomposity during a breach of discipline. 'Fifteen of us, fighting off boredom, formed a circle and started throwing a ration of German war-bread from one to the other in good rugger style. Presently some ass dropped a catch and kicked the bread to a companion. Almost immediately we were surrounded by the German guards and placed under arrest.'

The consequences were daunting. All fifteen British officers were put on trial in Berlin 'for insulting the German nation by kicking their war bread about'. They were eloquently defended by a general who spoke in German and perfect English. The courtroom was brimming with Germanic top brass. Sentence for all but one was seven days' solitary confinement, in darkened cells. The senior British officer, a Captain in the Gordon Highlanders, got ten days.

In the next cell to MacBryan was a chap called Kenneth Henderson who, by an odd coincidence, had been at the same private school. As a diversion to the silence and blackness, he continually knocked out messages in Morse code to Jack. 'I didn't understand a thing. Couldn't bear "Signals". Not clever enough. . .'

He came especially to like the Russian officers with whom at some stage he shared captivity. He listened for hours to them play their balalaikas and claimed they

169

were the kindest people he ever met. Some of them were extensive landowners, on the point of losing all their possessions in the political upheaval.

Russia's one-time landed gentry may have worn the dour expressions of their homeland, but they weren't averse, it appears, to flights of eroticism. They amused the British officers by telling them of a popular game the men liked to play before a meal. They would put a nubile girl under the table. She was encouraged 'to play with them'. Whoever smiled first ended up by paying for the dinner.

Who said MacBryan was born unlucky? His final nine months as a PoW were spent in Holland. By then he was general secretary of sports and pastimes for the officers and NCOs and he was allowed to enter two teams in the local cricket league. Jack found himself with pleasant dictatorial powers in matters of team selection. He grabbed the best players and his side won the league. The Dutch took their cricket seriously, of course, and the captain of All Holland had played for W. G. Grace's London Counties XI.

Mac lost his sword when he was taken prisoner. As he used to say many times: 'I'd have been quite incapable of using it against the enemy but it came in handy as a walking stick, until it got caught between some cobbles and a piece came off the point.'

The history of that sword makes a charming story. 'After my capture it was taken from me and eventually came into the possession of a German landowner who proudly added it to his collection of weapons. But at the end of the Second World War his property was occupied by the British troops. One of the officers recognized at once one of our infantry swords. By an extraordinary coincidence his father had been a friend of mine. He took the sword to Lord's and it was passed on to me. It's now in the Military Museum at Taunton, along with a cup which I won for tennis in an Anglo-Belgian tournament while I was a prisoner.'

When Jack landed back in this country, his father and

one of his brothers were waiting for him. He was starving but because of rationing there was nothing to eat. So, ever resourceful and dreaming again of the good times, he headed for the Piccadilly Grill. 'Had a hell of a meal, too – on my ration cards!'

He joined the RAF in the 1939-45 war and ended up a Squadron Leader. There was work with barrage balloons in the London area and he saw service in Canada before a posting in Blackpool where he helped to run the cricket.

Jack had an eye for a pretty girl and we should not ignore it. His linguistic flair – he was quite capable of reading a novel in French and had a passable grasp of several other languages – impressed his lady friends over the dinner table. He was a bit of a name-dropper. His sporting prowess was well known. He had the right connections. Peter Johnson may have implied that he was a bad tempered old so-and-so but in the company of an attractive companion he had an undeniable charm.

His marriage to Myra Thompson, a strikingly good-looking 'Gaiety Girl' took his friends by surprise. 'Tommy' was a singer. She had the presence that made male eyes turn. 'I just don't know why he married her – they had nothing much in common,' I was told. Jack, the young man supposedly always in charge of his emotions, was infatuated by Tommy's allure. All the well-meaning friends knew it wouldn't last. She went off with someone else.

There were several other close friendships, some no doubt platonic. He liked younger girls and in the case of one there were veiled, unsubstantiated rumours that she was his illegitimate daughter. In fact, he had no children.

One lasting and touching friendship was with a much younger woman who, herself, had a quite serious mental condition. They often met and up to his death had many chats on the phone. He befriended her with patience and compassion, to reveal qualities that many believed he never possessed.

Since the early 1960s he had lived at the home of Mrs Cecil Mackay, an intelligent and charming widow, who grew up at Weston-super-Mare and as a child watched Somerset play. Her father was a solicitor, friend of the Daniells and the other well-established cricketing families. Cecil as a child knew Jack vaguely. They met again by chance at the wedding of the grandson of John Daniell. She was then secretary of the Society of Genealogists. He went to stay with her, first in London and then in Cambridge. She handled him superbly, giving him the companionship for which he now yearned. She cooked his meals and encouraged him to talk incessantly about old friends and enemies. When he flew into a tantrum, she smiled to herself and ignored it. She had an engaging sense of humour. 'Jack loved to talk, mostly about himself. He had to be tactfully steered off the subject.'

She brought out the dry humour in him. One day she came in from the small, neatly kept back garden. 'I really do think sparrows are my favourite birds – I've just been watching them in fascination,' she told him.

He looked up. 'We must try and let them know, mustn't we.'

MacBryan had first taken up embroidery when a PoW – yet another creative way he used his time – and in the late years of his life, his 'sewing' was for him an absorbing form of therapy. Each piece of embroidery was researched and planned to the minutest detail. There were entries in the diary. His Wyvern, which he completed for the Somerset Exiles, now hangs in the Taunton pavilion. Past enmity had apparently been buried at last. I know that several letters were sent to him from the county headquarters in a bid to embrace him once more into the club.

The present officials' distant predecessors weren't going to be forgiven that easily for earlier slights and antagonisms. At the same time he was privately pleased that his name was recognized again at Taunton, in the same way that, with a hint of vanity, he was suddenly back in the public prints as 'England's oldest surviving Test cricketer', just ahead of Percy Fender.

He had an ulcer and made a good recovery. He had difficulty getting his clothes on but with defiant independence wouldn't let anyone, not even the district nurse, help him. He was always falling over. If one of the other lodgers wasn't around, Cecil would go out in the road and stop the first strong man passing by: 'Would you kindly come in a moment and pick up an old gentleman for me?' Jack would sniff at the seeming indignity but it didn't embarrass him a bit.

The prospect of wearing false teeth ruffled up his feathers far more. No one was going to put a denture in his mouth, even though all his teeth had fallen out.

'There was an awfully nice chap who'd set up as a dentist just round the corner,' said Cecil. She saw him in the garden and asked if she could bring Jack round for a fitting. 'I'll come round and see him,' said the accommodating dentist.

Mac's reaction was predictable. 'Come here, Cecil . . . this fellow you met in the road . . . well, are you sure he's properly qualified?'

Mrs Mackay is convinced Jack thought the dentist was one of those versatile quacks who used to go round the fairs taking out teeth at sixpence a time.

He died early in the morning on 14 July 1983. The funeral service was on his ninety-first birthday. There were fourteen mourners, including family, close friends and representatives from Jesus College and the Wyverns.

4

Subterfuge at the Olympics

J. C. W. MacBryan was Nigel Daniell's boyhood hero. He was 'a beautiful bat'. The strokes were so meticulously chiselled and fashioned. The light-blue cap and the neat, military walk to the wicket lent distinction. And, by jove, he came and stayed with the family at Weston-super-Mare.

Nigel was too young to detect any tensions or rivalries. But it did disappoint him that Mr MacBryan wasn't very interested in the children. 'I don't remember him ever really talking to me, unlike other members of the team . . . Tom Lowry, Dar Lyon, Guy Earle, Jim Bridges and Glasgie. Instead, Jack used to come and sit with us and talk to my mother whom, I was told, he rather fancied. We used to play cricket on the green near the home of Cecil Mackay's parents, the Beres, in the evening. I don't think that Jack ever once joined in.'

Although there is some evidence that MacBryan mellowed in his opinion of John Daniell in late years, the prickly relationship of the two is central to the story in this book. Nigel was a loyal son and a fair-minded one. I admired the way he rallied to the defence of his father when I wrote my biography of Harold Gimblett. So I asked him for a candid reassessment. His letter read:

I have been trying to think back, a very long time back, and I'm afraid I cannot recall any single amusing incident relating to Jack MacBryan. He was not, in any way, an amusing man. My recollections of him are early ones when we lived at Weston.

After the 1920s I do not think I crossed paths with him again until I was in my fifties, probably after my father had died, when he started writing to my mother, doing stock-exchange business with the family, and coming down to stay – at his own request, may I say. He was rather impossible at this time, smoking like a chimney, spilling ash everywhere and burning holes in the carpets.

I really do not know how he felt towards my father but my mother said he did not like him very much. This, I feel, applied to most other members of the Somerset XI. He was a bit of a loner, I suppose. . .

It was a classic case of the unrealities of hero worship. The last time Nigel saw Jack MacBryan was in the late 1960s when he invited himself down to stay with him at Taunton. 'We picked him up from the station on Good Friday and were rather grateful to put him back on the train on Easter Monday. He did take us out to lunch at the Grand Atlantic, Weston on the Sunday. But I have to admit he was by now pretty boring company.'

I redress the balance with two more tales, perhaps equally revealing, on the Daniell-MacBryan relationship.

Sidney Considine was not perhaps the best batsman ever to play for Somerset. In just under ninety matches for the county, spanned over sixteen years, he was capable however of unfurling a cover boundary of quite poetic quality. MacBryan was batting with him at Bournemouth and the off-drives were racing away with almost indecent regularity.

The more circumspect JCW became perplexed. 'Consy' was going like a runaway horse. The shots were going away like a bullet but would the rush of blood be his undoing? MacBryan quite consciously began to farm the bowling.

At lunch, John Daniell approached him with a look

of unmistakable rebuke. 'You should be ashamed of yourself taking the bowling when he was playing so much better than you.'

It was a public reprimand. The verbal sting over the two players' respective merits – batsmen who as everyone knew were not remotely in the same class – hurt.

'All I was trying to do,' he assured me many years later, 'was to help "Consy". I didn't want him to go too fast!'

A few years earlier, in the August of 1920, MacBryan received an invitation to play hockey for his country in the Olympic Games, being held in Antwerp. He was elated and when he arrived at the Somerset ground he was told by his captain, Daniell: 'What the hell do you want to do that for? I've now got to find another player.'

That was all, according to the aggrieved Mac: no word of praise or slap on the back. 'Anyway, I went,' he adds in dismissive tones.

There was an amusing and so far unpublicized sequel to those Games. A South African called Rudd won the 100 and 200 metres, but most of the British competitors were ushered off home as soon as their events were over. MacBryan was still there, however, at the time of the prize-giving by the King of the Belgians.

'For some reason, probably because I also had very dark hair, I was discreetly asked to take Rudd's place. The name was called out and up I went, a party to the subterfuge.

'The King shook my hand and said he was honoured to meet me because South African troops had occupied a small area of Belgium for the whole of the war which had just ended. I acknowledged with courtesy. My phoney identity was never suspected.'

Jealousies existed in the Somerset amateurs' dressing room back in the twenties. 'John Daniell was jealous of me,' JCW repeatedly told me. 'Jack was jealous of my father,' Nigel told me. Maybe there was more than an element of truth in both succinct statements. If we add the names of Peter Johnson and Jack White to the cauldron, we can only imagine, with the mischief of hindsight, the dramatic possibilities of the interaction.

MacBryan's mentor, Sammy Woods, on whom he lavished so much idolatry, was supposed to find rather less favour with Daniell. 'He looked upon Sam as a mere boozer', though I find it hard to accept that judgment.

'Sam Woods was adored by all the ladies. He kept them entertained with a limitless fund of stories, often about cricket of which they knew nothing. On the days he walked to the county ground from Bridgwater, he stopped on the way to talk to all the farmers' wives. The farmers didn't object – they felt rather flattered. I'm not too sure what John Daniell and some of his chums made of all that attention.'

But those same chums in the team were just as hard to fathom, he contended, when it came to social chit-chat. It irked him that never once did a so-called educated member of the side ask him about his varied experiences during three and a half years as a PoW. 'I had dealings with French, Belgians, Russians, Poles and Serbs – and no one was the least bit interested. What DID interest them, I used to wonder?

'It wasn't until we played a match against Leicestershire, captained by George Fowke, that the Somerset amateurs were told about some of the things that happened in Holland. Major Fowke was the skipper of our team in the Dutch League. He told my team mates a thing or two, I can promise you.'

This was never going to be a homage to Jack MacBryan. He'd have been horrified by such an idea. He was never a hypocrite. Those on whom he turned his scorn all admitted he did it to their face. He quarrelled with his relatives and sister Ivy, for instance, 'took it very calmly'. He went into frightful rages about falling standards or resurrected animosities. 'If you took no notice, it was quickly all over and he'd forgotten all about it,' said Mrs Cecil Mackay.

Like Charlie Parker and Cecil Parkin, he had a streak

of unbridled sadism. He had no inhibitions about rubbing people up the wrong way. Bill Greswell, later to become president of Somerset, made his reputation for his wickedly late in-swing. It was something new and he began to reap the wickets. MacBryan walked up to him: 'Players are getting familiar with your swing now, Bill. You won't find it so easy in future.' Greswell, he admits, got very annoyed.

Some of his colleagues found him rather bombastic. He could be pedantic. 'There's a general error in the much repeated joke that Tom Lowry got into the Somerset side because he came from Wellington – and the authorities thought it was the Wellington in Somerset and not New Zealand. Well, Lowry was a New Zealander but didn't come from Wellington. Peter Randall Johnson did.' Nice one, Mac.

I am coming to the end. I have written about him at such length not simply because he was an exceptional cricketer who, like Charlie, should have played more for England. He worked hard to show me his bad points. 'I really was rather a bastard, an old misery,' he seemed to be telling me on every visit.

Much of the evidence went a long way to substantiate the self-indictment. I can only say that for some odd reason I acquired a growing affection for him. The body was shrunken, as he hunched in his dressing gown, but the eyes continued to spark. His words were more evocative than a sepia photograph.

He was a sophisticate who'd flirted with the pages of Debrett. He wasn't a Blimp or a High Tory. Some thought he was cussedly left of centre. It pleased him to go out an enigma. He was gruff, grumpy and at times marvellously gentle. He despised sentimentality but wallowed in the story told by Gubby Allen about the way his military sword was rediscovered during an MCC tour of West Germany in 1946.

Cecil Mackay gave him a television set and he never switched it on. Brian Johnson used to wish him a happy birthday if it coincided with a Test match. Jack would be told about it, pretended to sniff at the mere thought of such nonsense and was immeasurably thrilled.

Not long before he died I asked him on impulse whether he would like to have another look at Box. He was in his dressing gown at the time and becoming progressively more immobile by the day. It wasn't the brightest idea I had ever come up with.

His eyes lit up. Yes, somehow or other he would make the journey from Cambridge to his old home at Kingsdown House, just outside Bath.

I drove back to Bristol, regretting my suggestion because it was so fraught with impracticabilities. Jack, almost daily, wrote a succession of wildly enthusiastic letters. 'I'm putting the organization in your hands, old chap. You're the manager. Find me a decent hotel.' He was talking in endearing cricketing parlance.

We arranged a provisional date and I started ringing round the hotels in Bath. Jack, hollow-cheeked and still in his dressing gown, was planning to take not only Cecil but another girlfriend with him. It was going to be quite a party. 'I'll take you all round the house ∴ . . . and the little local golf-course . . . and the Downs nearby where I played my first organized game of cricket at the age of seven . . . No, I don't think we'll go down to Taunton . . . No, definitely not.'

Not Taunton – or Box. He died a fortnight later.

Bibliography

C. W. L. PARKER:
E. W. Swanton, *History of Cricket, Vol. 2*
Walter Hammond, *Cricket My Destiny*
Sir Pelham Warner, *The Fight for the Ashes in 1926*
R. E. S. Wyatt, *Three Straight Sticks*
I. Rosenwater, *Sir Donald Bradman*
Michael Page, *Bradman: The Illustrated Biography*
Grahame Parker, *Gloucestershire Road*
Sir Neville Cardus, *Playfair Cricket Monthly* (April 1970)
Adrian Crowley, *The Cricketer* (April 1971)
A. A. Thomson, *Cricketers of My Time*

C. H. PARKIN:
Sir Neville Cardus, *The Summer Game*
—, *The Playfair Cardus, 1963*
C. H. Parkin, *Cricket Triumphs and Troubles*
R. C. Robertson-Glasgow, *Crusoe on Cricket*
A. E. R. Gilligan, *Sussex Cricket 1933*
L. Duckworth, *The Story of Warwickshire Cricket*
J. Marshall, *Old Trafford*
R. Pogson, *Lancashire – The County Cricket Series*
P. Murphy, *'Tiger' Smith*
Derek Birley, *The Willow Wand*
A. A. Thomson, *The War of the Roses*

J. C. W. MACBRYAN:
R. C. Robertson-Glasgow, *46 Not Out*
—, *Cricket Prints*
Bill Andrews, *The Hand That Bowled Bradman*

Newspapers:
The Times (12 July 1926)
Western Daily Press (same date)
Gloucestershire Echo (1930)

Wisden
The Cricketer
Wisden Cricket Monthly

Index

181